Developing Skills in
ALGEBRA ONE

Harold Taylor ■ Loretta Taylor

Book C

DALE SEYMOUR PUBLICATIONS

Cover Design: Michael Rogondino
Technical Illustrations: Pat Rogondino

Order Number DS01443
ISBN 0-86651-223-3

**DALE
SEYMOUR
PUBLICATIONS**
P.O. BOX 10888
PALO ALTO, CA 94303

defgh-MA-9543210

CONTENTS

Introduction   v

Ratio and Proportion

Ratio *(numerical)*   1
Ratio *(verbal)*   3
Proportion *(numerical)*   5
Proportion *(verbal)*   7
Ratio and Proportion   9
Equations with Fractions *(monomial numerators)*   13
Equations with Fractions *(binomial numerators)*   17
Equations with Fractions *(mixed expressions)*   19
Equations with Fractions *(decimal fractions)*   21
Fractional Equations   23
Investment Problems   27
Mixture Problems   29
Motion Problems   33
Rate of Work Problems   37

Linear Equations

Equations in Two Variables   41
Graphing Linear Equations   45
Graphing in the Coordinate Plane   49
Slope of a Line   51
Equations in Two Variables *(slope and intercept)*   53
Equations in Two Variables *(slope and point, two points)*   55
Equations in Two Variables *(graphs)*   57

Systems of Equations

Solving Equations with Two Variables *(graphing)*   59
Solving Equations with Two Variables *(substitution)*   61
Solving Equations with Two Variables *(addition or subtraction)*   63

(over)

Number Problems   67
Perimeter Problems   69
Age Problems   71
Digit Problems   73
Money Problems   75
Motion Problems   77
Temperature Problems   79
Mixture Problems   81
Miscellaneous Word Problems   83

Inequalities and Absolute Value

Solving Inequalities   87
Solving Absolute Value Equations   91
Absolute Value Inequalities   95
Graphing Linear Inequalities   97
Solving Systems of Inequalities   99

Answers   103

INTRODUCTION

In order to master algebra, most students need a great deal of practice—practice allowing them to discover mathematical patterns, to make generalizations, and to consolidate their mathematical learning—practice that helps them see and understand the workings of algebra. Algebra textbooks, by their very nature, cannot provide the quantity of problems necessary for a beginning algebra course. In order to cover the complete range of problems related to a topic, most textbook exercise sets move very quickly from simple to complex problems, giving only a few of those in-between bread-and-butter problems that students need. As a result, algebra teachers are continually looking for problems to supplement their texts.

About the Series

Developing Skills in Algebra One was created primarily to help teachers in their search for extra algebra problems. The series was not designed to be a classroom text, rather it is a back-up resource containing problems for class examples, chalkboard work, quizzes, test preparation, and extra practice. *Developing Skills in Algebra One* is a four-book series of reproducible worksheets that provides extensive practice in all the work covered in the traditional first high school course in algebra.

Book A starts at the beginning of the school year with exercises in simplifying numerical expressions, and continues through to simple equations in one variable.

Book B includes operations with polynomials, factoring polynomials, solving polynomial equations, and working with rational expressions.

Book C covers ratio, proportion, graphing linear equations, solving systems of linear equations, plus inequalities and absolute value equations.

Book D completes the algebra one course with roots and radicals, quadratic equations, and analysis of quadratic functions.

By design, the books in the *Developing Skills in Algebra One* series are appropriate for use in any algebra one course, whether it is taught in ninth grade, tenth grade, seventh or eighth grade, or in a two-year algebra program. The books also provide review work for second-year algebra students, practice for students studying high school algebra at the college level, and exercises for adults reviewing algebra on their own.

Pick-and-Choose Pages

Book C is the third book in the *Developing Skills in Algebra* series. It contains 102 worksheets with more than 2500 problems that you can duplicate and use with your students. There is no required order for presenting the exercises in this book but, for maximum convenience, the worksheets are arranged sequentially, concept by concept. You may choose to select worksheets from the book as back-up for your algebra lessons. You might assign a worksheet to a single student who needs practice in a specific skill. Or, you may decide to keep certain pages as your own personal resource of problems on a particular topic. The contents in the front of this book and the labels at the top of each worksheet page will help you identify the exercises that best meet your needs.

Paired Worksheets and Exercises

As you glance through this book, you will discover that the worksheets come in pairs; there are at least two parallel worksheets for every concept so that students can learn on one set of problems and practice on the next. Several pairs of worksheets are included for particularly troublesome topics. Each pair of worksheets practices only one or two specific skills (noted at the top left of the pages), carefully sequenced and organized. Most worksheet exercises are also paired, by odds and evens, to allow for two-day assignments or for practice and testing. And, clear simple worksheet instructions along with handwritten samples of the exercises allow students to get right to work with a minimum of fuss.

Checking Work

In order to provide a quantity of problems—enough problems on a page to make it worth copying—and in order to give you complete coverage of algebra topics, we have limited the amount of workspace allowed for some exercises. We suggest that you have students show all their work on separate sheets of paper, but transfer their answers to the worksheets. You (or your students) will have a quick way to check answers as well as access to the work you must see to diagnose students' errors of understanding.

You will find answers to every problem in this book. The answers are located after the worksheet pages.

About Practice

Practice is an important part of learning, but it's not the only part. Practice makes sense only after instruction and demonstrated understanding. To help students master algebra, we must aim for a regular and consistent blend of practice with meaningful instruction, taking pains to individualize practice as much as possible. *Developing Skills in Algebra One* is one tool you can use to achieve that goal, but it is just a tool. The hard work and dedication are up to you and your students.

Developing Skills in

ALGEBRA ONE

Ratio

Name _____

Date _____ Period _____

Write each ratio in lowest terms. Assume domains include only values that give nonzero denominators.

1. $\dfrac{5}{10}$ $\dfrac{1}{2}$ **2.** $\dfrac{7}{21}$ _____

3. $\dfrac{4}{10}$ _____   **4.** $\dfrac{12}{18}$ _____

5. $\dfrac{9}{24}$ _____   **6.** $\dfrac{15}{20}$ _____

7. $\dfrac{35}{42}$ _____   **8.** $\dfrac{24}{30}$ _____

9. $\dfrac{3x^2y^3}{5xy^4}$ _____   **10.** $\dfrac{2xy^5}{3x^2y^4}$ _____

11. $\dfrac{12x^3y}{30xy^4}$ _____   **12.** $\dfrac{15x^2y^4}{40xy^3}$ _____

13. $\dfrac{x^2 - 10x + 21}{x^2 - 5x - 14}$ _____   **14.** $\dfrac{x^2 - x - 12}{x^2 - 6x + 8}$ _____

15. $\dfrac{2x^2 - 13x + 15}{2x^2 + x - 6}$ _____   **16.** $\dfrac{3x^2 + 11x - 4}{3x^2 - 7x + 2}$ _____

Find the ratio of y to x. $\left(\text{Solve for } \dfrac{y}{x}\right)$.

17. $4x = 9y$ $\dfrac{4}{9}$ **18.** $7x = 10y$ _____

19. $12x = 15y$ _____   **20.** $18x = 24y$ _____

21. $4x - 2y = 7y$ _____   **22.** $5x - 3y = 4y$ _____

23. $3y + 2x = 4x$ _____   **24.** $5y + 4x = 7x$ _____

25. $x - y = 7y$ _____   **26.** $y - x = 2x$ _____

27. $x + 2y = 3(x + y)$ _____   **28.** $3y + x = 5(x - y)$ _____

Ratio

Name _____

Date _____ Period _____

Write each ratio in lowest terms. Assume domains include only values that give nonzero denominators.

1. $\dfrac{4}{16}$ $\dfrac{1}{4}$ 2. $\dfrac{5}{15}$ _____

3. $\dfrac{6}{14}$ _____   4. $\dfrac{14}{21}$ _____

5. $\dfrac{16}{28}$ _____   6. $\dfrac{10}{25}$ _____

7. $\dfrac{24}{54}$ _____   8. $\dfrac{24}{32}$ _____

9. $\dfrac{7x^3y}{10x^2y^2}$ _____   10. $\dfrac{5x^2y^3}{8x^2y^2}$ _____

11. $\dfrac{14x^5y^2}{24x^2y^4}$ _____   12. $\dfrac{20x^2y^4}{45x^4y^6}$ _____

13. $\dfrac{x^2 - x - 30}{x^2 + 9x + 20}$ _____   14. $\dfrac{x^2 - 9x + 14}{x^2 + 2x - 63}$ _____

15. $\dfrac{2x^2 + x - 15}{x^2 + 7x + 12}$ _____   16. $\dfrac{3x^2 + 11x + 6}{3x^2 + 17x + 10}$ _____

Find the ratio of y to x. $\left(\text{Solve for } \dfrac{y}{x}\right)$.

17. $5x = 7y$ $\dfrac{5}{7}$ 18. $9x = 8y$ _____

19. $9x = 15y$ _____   20. $12x = 30y$ _____

21. $5x - 3y = 7y$ _____   22. $7x - 2y = 10y$ _____

23. $5y + 3x = 11x$ _____   24. $9y + 3x = 9x$ _____

25. $x + y = 9x$ _____   26. $y - x = 5y$ _____

27. $2x + y = 4(x - y)$ _____   28. $5y + 2x = 7(2x + y)$ _____

Developing Skills in Algebra   Book C

Ratio

Solve. Express each ratio as a fraction reduced to lowest terms.

1. Pam has 3 red marbles and 5 blue ones. Write the ratio of red marbles to blue marbles.

$\frac{3}{5}$

2. Joan has 10 nickels and 12 dimes. Write the ratio of nickels to dimes.

3. In a class of 29 males and females there are 12 females. Write the ratio of males to females.

4. In a box of 31 pens and pencils there are 13 pencils. Write the ratio of pens to pencils.

5. The length of a rectangle is 27 centimeters and the width is 18 centimeters. Write the ratio of length to width.

6. The base of a parallelogram is 21 centimeters and the height is 14 centimeters. Write the ratio of the base to the height.

7. The perimeter of a rectangle is 28 km and the length is 4 km more than the width. Write the ratio of the length to the width.

8. The perimeter of a rectangle is 34 km and the length is 5 km more than the width. Write the ratio of the length to the width.

9. Two numbers are in a ratio of 1 to 5. Their sum is 30. Find the numbers.

10. Two numbers are in a ratio of 1 to 7. Their sum is 56. Find the numbers.

11. Two numbers are in a ratio 2 to 3. Their sum is 50. Find the numbers.

12. Two numbers are in a ratio 4 to 5. Their sum is 63. Find the numbers.

Ratio

Date _____ Period _____

Solve. Express each ratio as a fraction reduced to lowest terms.

1. The ratio of two numbers is 8 to 9. Their difference is 7. What are the numbers?

x = one number $x - \frac{8}{9}x = 7$ The numbers are
$\frac{8}{9}x$ = the other number $\frac{1}{9}x = 7$ 63 and 56.
$x = 63$

2. The ratio of two numbers is 8 to 9. Their difference is 10. What are the numbers?

3. The ratio of the number of nickels to dimes is 4 to 5. The total number of nickels and dimes is 81. Find the number of each kind of coin.

4. The ratio of the number of nickels to quarters is 6 to 5. The total number of nickels and quarters is 22. Find the number of each kind of coin.

5. The ratio of sand to cement is 6 to 5. How much cement is in a 220 kg mixture?

6. The ratio of paint to thinner is 8 to 1. How much thinner should be used with 10 L of paint?

7. The ratio of the number of quarters to dimes is 3 to 4. The total value of the money is $13.80. How many quarters are there?

8. The difference between the value of some quarters and nickels is 90 cents. The ratio of the number of quarters to nickels is 1 to 2. Find the number of each kind of coin.

9. The ratio of male students to female students is 10 to 13. There are 1219 students in all. How many are female?

10. The ratio of female teachers to male teachers is 7 to 5. If there is a total of 48 teachers, how many are male?

Proportion

Write the cross products for each proportion.

1. $\dfrac{a}{b} = \dfrac{c}{d}$ $ad = cb$ 2. $\dfrac{a}{c} = \dfrac{b}{d}$ _____

3. $\dfrac{m}{n} = \dfrac{p}{q}$ _____   4. $\dfrac{m}{p} = \dfrac{n}{q}$ _____

Solve each proportion for x.

5. $\dfrac{x}{3} = \dfrac{5}{9}$ $x = \dfrac{5}{3}$ 6. $\dfrac{x}{6} = \dfrac{3}{8}$ _____

7. $\dfrac{x}{7} = \dfrac{3}{14}$ _____   8. $\dfrac{x}{4} = \dfrac{5}{6}$ _____

9. $\dfrac{x+2}{5} = \dfrac{x+3}{7}$ _____   10. $\dfrac{2x}{3} = \dfrac{x+2}{6}$ _____

11. $\dfrac{x-4}{3} = \dfrac{x+3}{5}$ _____   12. $\dfrac{3x-2}{5} = \dfrac{x+2}{3}$ _____

13. $\dfrac{x+6}{x-5} = \dfrac{x+2}{x-4}$ _____   14. $\dfrac{4x+3}{2x-3} = \dfrac{6x-5}{3x+2}$ _____

15. $\dfrac{x+3}{x-2} = \dfrac{x+7}{x+1}$ _____   16. $\dfrac{2x+1}{x-2} = \dfrac{2x+1}{x+2}$ _____

17. $\dfrac{3x+1}{4x+3} = \dfrac{x+1}{x+3}$ _____   18. $\dfrac{2x+1}{5x+4} = \dfrac{11x+7}{49x+5}$ _____

19. $\dfrac{x+1}{x+3} = \dfrac{2x-1}{x+7}$ _____   20. $\dfrac{x+2}{3x-4} = \dfrac{2x+1}{2x+4}$ _____

21. $\dfrac{x+1}{x+3} = \dfrac{3x-5}{2x+6}$ _____   22. $\dfrac{x+2}{3x-1} = \dfrac{3x+1}{5x+1}$ _____

23. $\dfrac{2x-5}{x+2} = \dfrac{3x-5}{3x-1}$ _____   24. $\dfrac{x-3}{x-1} = \dfrac{x+3}{2x+3}$ _____

Proportion

Name _____

Date _____ Period _____

Write the cross products for each proportion.

1. $\dfrac{x}{y} = \dfrac{z}{v}$ $xv = yz$

2. $\dfrac{5x}{3y} = \dfrac{7k}{2s}$ _____

3. $\dfrac{r}{s} = \dfrac{k}{t}$ _____

4. $\dfrac{7y}{18} = \dfrac{2x}{9}$ _____

Solve each proportion for x.

5. $\dfrac{x}{18} = \dfrac{2}{9}$ $x = 4$

6. $\dfrac{3x}{5} = \dfrac{9}{4}$ _____

7. $\dfrac{4x}{9} = \dfrac{6}{7}$ _____

8. $\dfrac{5x}{11} = \dfrac{5}{2}$ _____

9. $\dfrac{5x}{8} = \dfrac{x-4}{4}$ _____

10. $\dfrac{7x}{4} = \dfrac{2x+3}{4}$ _____

11. $\dfrac{x-2}{3} = \dfrac{2x+4}{4}$ _____

12. $\dfrac{2x+3}{5} = \dfrac{x+1}{6}$ _____

13. $\dfrac{x-1}{x+2} = \dfrac{3x-2}{8x}$ _____

14. $\dfrac{x-6}{x-2} = \dfrac{x-5}{x+3}$ _____

15. $\dfrac{x-3}{2x-5} = \dfrac{x+3}{4x}$ _____

16. $\dfrac{x-7}{x-2} = \dfrac{x-5}{x+5}$ _____

17. $\dfrac{2x-11}{2x-8} = \dfrac{x+2}{2x}$ _____

18. $\dfrac{2x-3}{3x-4} = \dfrac{4x-1}{5x+4}$ _____

19. $\dfrac{x-7}{x-6} = \dfrac{2x-11}{x+2}$ _____

20. $\dfrac{x-9}{x-8} = \dfrac{x-1}{2x-7}$ _____

21. $\dfrac{2x-1}{2x+2} = \dfrac{3x+3}{5x-1}$ _____

22. $\dfrac{x-2}{2x+1} = \dfrac{x+3}{4x+2}$ _____

23. $\dfrac{2x+2}{5x-3} = \dfrac{7x+3}{13x-3}$ _____

24. $\dfrac{x+5}{2x-2} = \dfrac{3x+1}{4x-4}$ _____

6

Proportion

Write a proportion for each problem and then solve it.

1. If one automobile used 18 gallons of gasoline while a second used 12 gallons, how many gallons of gasoline did the second automobile use when the first one used 39 gallons? *The second*

x = *am't gas second used when first used 39 gal.* $\qquad \frac{12}{18} = \frac{x}{39} \qquad 18x = 468 \qquad$ *automobile*

$\qquad \qquad \qquad \qquad \qquad \qquad \qquad \qquad \qquad \qquad \qquad x = 26 \qquad$ *used 26 gallons.*

2. The length of a rectangle is 6 centimeters more than the width. The ratio of the length to the width is 5 to 3. Find the dimensions of the rectangle.

3. The ratio of the areas of two triangles is 8 to 5. The altitude of one triangle is 5 centimeters more than the altitude of the other while the bases are each equal to 10 centimeters. Find the altitude of each triangle.

4. Gary has $500 more invested at 12% than he has invested at 10%. The ratio of the amount invested at 12% to what is invested at 10% is 7 to 5. How much does he have invested at 10%?

5. According to the scale on a map of the United States, 5 centimeters equals 200 km. If Los Angeles is 540 km from San Francisco, how many centimeters apart would the two cities be on the map?

6. If the ratio of $x^2 - 16$ to $x^2 + 7x + 12$ is 3 to 2, find x.

7. In a basketball game the ratio of the scores between the Bears and the Bobcats was 13 to 9. If the Bears scored 78 points, how many points did the Bobcats score?

8. If the ratio of the cost of one motorcycle helmet to another is 12 to 7 and if the more expensive helmet costs $102, what is the price of the less expensive one?

9. The length of a rectangle is 8 more than twice the width. The ratio of length to width is 12 to 5. Find the length and the width of the rectangle.

10. The ratio between the acceleration rates of two automobiles is 4 to 3. The car with the faster rate can go from 0 km/h to 80 km/h in 9 seconds. How long will it take the slower car to go from 0 km/h to 80 km/h?

Name _____

Date _____ Period _____

Write a proportion for each problem and solve.

1. If one automobile used 16 L of gasoline while a second used 26 L, how many liters of gasoline did the first automobile use when the second one used 65 L?

x = am't gas first auto used when second used 65 L $\frac{16}{26} = \frac{x}{65}$ $26x = 1040$ $x = 40$ The first automobile used 40L of gasoline.

2. The length of a rectangle is 4 centimeters less than three times the width. The ratio of the length to the width is 7 to 3. Find the dimensions of the rectangle.

3. The ratio of the areas of two triangles is 4 to 3. If their bases are each 14 centimeters and if the area of the smaller triangle is 147 centimeters^2, find the area of the large triangle.

4. Lysa had $2100 invested at 14% and a smaller amount invested at 11%. If the ratio of the two investments is 10 to 7, how much did she have invested at the lower rate?

5. The scale on a map of the United States is: 6 centimeters equals 150 kilometers. On the map, Denver and Colorado Springs are 4 centimeters apart. Find the distance between the two cities.

6. If the ratio of $x^2 + 2x + 1$ to $x^2 + 10x + 9$ is 7 to 8, find x.

7. In a football game the ratio of the scores between the Knights and the Falcons was 3 to 2. If the Falcons scored 28 points, how many points did the Knights score?

8. The ratio of the cost of one automobile to another is 5 to 2. If the more expensive one costs $24,000, find the price of the less expensive one.

9. The length of a rectangle is 4 more than the width. The ratio of length to width is 5 to 7. Find the length and the width of the rectangle.

10. The ratio between the acceleration rates of two automobiles is 5 to 3. The car with the faster rate can go from 0 km/h to 80 km/h in 9 seconds. How long will it take the slower car to go from 0 km/h to 80 km/h?

Developing Skills in Algebra   Book C

Ratio and Proportion

Name _____

Date _____ Period _____

Write each ratio in lowest terms.

1. $\dfrac{13}{39}$ $\dfrac{1}{3}$

2. $\dfrac{21}{91}$ _____

3. $\dfrac{14x^4y^3}{6x^5y^5}$ _____

4. $\dfrac{2x^2 - 25x - 42}{2x^2 - 11x - 21}$ _____

Find the ratio of y to x.

5. $7x = 12y$ $\dfrac{7}{12}$

6. $20x = 42y$ _____

7. $5x - 3y = 9y$ _____

8. $7y + 2x = -7x$ _____

9. $\dfrac{2x + y}{x - y} = 3$ _____

10. $\dfrac{2x + y}{x - y} = \dfrac{2x + y}{x + 2y}$ _____

Solve.

11. There is a total of 15 cards, 6 of which are red with the remainder black. What is the ratio of red cards to black cards?

12. Two numbers are in a ratio of 8 to 7. Their sum is 90. What are the numbers?

Write the cross products.

13. $\dfrac{r^2s}{t} = \dfrac{t^5}{rs^2}$ _____

14. $\dfrac{mn^2}{pq} = \dfrac{p^2q^3}{mn}$ _____

Solve each proportion for x.

15. $\dfrac{x - 7}{x - 6} = \dfrac{2x - 14}{x - 1}$ $x = 11 \text{ or } 7$

16. $\dfrac{x + 2}{2x - 8} = \dfrac{2x + 6}{3x - 4}$ _____

17. $\dfrac{x + 2}{7} = \dfrac{x - 3}{5}$ _____

18. $\dfrac{x}{11} = \dfrac{24}{4}$ _____

19. $\dfrac{x - 4}{x - 3} = \dfrac{x + 5}{2x + 2}$ _____

20. $\dfrac{x - 5}{x - 2} = \dfrac{2x - 10}{x + 6}$ _____

Developing Skills in Algebra   Book C

Ratio and Proportion

Name _____

Date _____ Period _____

Write each ratio in lowest terms.

1. $\dfrac{28}{42}$ $\dfrac{2}{3}$ 2. $\dfrac{13}{91}$ _____

3. $\dfrac{26x^5y^3}{13x^3y^2}$ _____   4. $\dfrac{2x^2 - 5x + 3}{4x^2 + x - 5}$ _____

Find the ratio of y to x.

5. $8y = 28x$ _____   6. $17x = 21y$ _____

7. $7x + 2y = 12x$ _____   8. $11y - 3x = -8x$ _____

9. $\dfrac{3x - y}{2x + 3y} = 7$ _____   10. $\dfrac{3x + 2y}{x - y} = \dfrac{3x - y}{x + 2y}$ _____

Solve.

11. An auto dealer has 162 cars on his lot. Seventy-two of the cars are solid colored and the remainder are two-toned. What is the ratio of solid colored cars to two-toned cars?

12. Two numbers are in a ratio of 7 to 5. Their difference is 32. What are the numbers?

Write the cross products.

13. $\dfrac{kx^2}{y^2} = \dfrac{k^2x}{y}$ _____   14. $\dfrac{a^2b^2}{cd^3} = \dfrac{ab^3}{cd^3}$ _____

Solve each proportion for x.

15. $\dfrac{x - 2}{x + 1} = \dfrac{2x + 1}{4x - 4}$ $x = 7 \text{ or } \frac{1}{2}$ 16. $\dfrac{2x + 2}{3x + 1} = \dfrac{7x - 2}{6x + 2}$ _____

17. $\dfrac{2x - 1}{3} = \dfrac{x + 2}{5}$ _____   18. $\dfrac{13}{x} = \dfrac{21}{42}$ _____

19. $\dfrac{2x - 3}{3x - 1} = \dfrac{2x + 3}{7x + 3}$ _____   20. $\dfrac{2x - 1}{x + 1} = \dfrac{x + 2}{5x + 1}$ _____

Developing Skills in Algebra   Book C

Ratio and Proportion

Name _____

Date _____ Period _____

Write each ratio in lowest terms.

1. $\dfrac{39}{65}$ $\dfrac{3}{5}$

2. $\dfrac{85}{51}$ _____

3. $\dfrac{24x^4y^2}{3xy^3}$ _____

4. $\dfrac{10x^2 + x - 3}{6x^2 + 7x - 5}$ _____

Find the ratio of y to x.

5. $8y = 4x$ _____

6. $7x = 42y$ _____

7. $8y + 3x = 14y$ _____

8. $13x - 8x = 10y$ _____

9. $\dfrac{8x - y}{2y} = \dfrac{1}{4}$ _____

10. $\dfrac{4x - 3y}{x + 2y} = \dfrac{4x + 2y}{x - y}$ _____

Solve.

11. The perimeter of a rectangle is 32 km. The length is 4 km more than the width. Write the ratio of the length to the width.

12. The base of a parallelogram is 27 centimeters. The height is 6 centimeters less than $\dfrac{2}{3}$ of the base. Write the ratio of the base to the height.

Write the cross products.

13. $\dfrac{xy^5}{ab^2} = \dfrac{a^3b}{x^2y^2}$ _____

14. $\dfrac{m^2n^3}{xy} = \dfrac{x^3y^2}{mn^5}$ _____

Solve each proportion for x.

15. $\dfrac{2x + 1}{3x - 2} = \dfrac{5x - 2}{4x + 4}$ $x = 0$ or 4

16. $\dfrac{x + 1}{5x - 2} = \dfrac{2x + 2}{8x}$ _____

17. $\dfrac{2x - 1}{5} = \dfrac{x - 5}{3}$ _____

18. $\dfrac{8}{9} = \dfrac{24}{x}$ _____

19. $\dfrac{x - 2}{2x - 6} = \dfrac{2x + 1}{4x - 4}$ _____

20. $\dfrac{2x - 15}{x - 5} = \dfrac{x + 3}{x + 7}$ _____

Developing Skills in Algebra Book C

Ratio and Proportion

Name _____

Date _____ Period _____

Write each ratio in lowest terms.

1. $\dfrac{75}{105}$ $\dfrac{5}{7}$ _____

2. $\dfrac{35}{140}$ _____

3. $\dfrac{16x^4y^3}{80x^2y}$ _____

4. $\dfrac{6x^2 - 11x - 65}{3x^2 - 16x + 13}$ _____

Find the ratio of y to x.

5. $8x = 15y$ _____

6. $32y = 40x$ _____

7. $8x + 3y = 19y$ _____

8. $11y - 5x = 22y$ _____

9. $\dfrac{5x - 2y}{2x - 3y} = 11$ _____

10. $\dfrac{x + 2y}{2x + y} = \dfrac{4x - y}{8x + 2y}$ _____

Solve.

11. Two numbers are in a ratio of 6 to 5. Their sum is 121. Find the numbers.

12. Two numbers are in a ratio of 11 to 9. Their difference is 54. Find the numbers.

Write the cross products.

13. $\dfrac{ab}{rst} = \dfrac{r^2s^2}{a^3}$ _____

14. $\dfrac{mno^2}{kx} = \dfrac{k^2x^2}{m^2n^2p}$ _____

Solve each proportion for x.

15. $\dfrac{3x - 3}{2x + 1} = \dfrac{4x}{5x - 1}$ $x = \frac{1}{7} \text{ or } 3$ _____

16. $\dfrac{x - 2}{x - 1} = \dfrac{2x - 4}{x + 9}$ _____

17. $\dfrac{2x - 1}{11} = \dfrac{3x + 2}{7}$ _____

18. $\dfrac{17}{12} = \dfrac{x}{60}$ _____

19. $\dfrac{x - 3}{x - 1} = \dfrac{2x - 6}{3x - 14}$ _____

20. $\dfrac{x - 6}{x - 4} = \dfrac{2x - 5}{2x + 1}$ _____

Developing Skills in Algebra Book C

Name _____

Date _____ Period _____

Solve.

1. $\dfrac{x}{3} + \dfrac{x}{4} = 7$ *x = 12*   **2.** $\dfrac{x}{5} + \dfrac{x}{3} = 24$ _____

3. $\dfrac{x}{5} - \dfrac{x}{6} = 2$ _____   **4.** $\dfrac{x}{4} - \dfrac{x}{12} = 20$ _____

5. $\dfrac{x}{7} + \dfrac{x}{3} = -20$ _____   **6.** $\dfrac{x}{9} + \dfrac{x}{3} = 28$ _____

7. $\dfrac{x}{9} - \dfrac{x}{11} = 24$ _____   **8.** $\dfrac{x}{7} - \dfrac{x}{12} = 55$ _____

9. $\dfrac{x}{6} + \dfrac{x}{7} = 91$ _____   **10.** $\dfrac{x}{14} + \dfrac{x}{20} = 68$ _____

11. $\dfrac{3x}{2} + \dfrac{7x}{3} = 46$ _____   **12.** $\dfrac{3x}{7} - \dfrac{4x}{5} = 26$ _____

13. $\dfrac{5x}{8} + \dfrac{4x}{3} = -94$ _____   **14.** $\dfrac{4x}{3} + \dfrac{5x}{8} = 47$ _____

15. $\dfrac{-11x}{7} + \dfrac{6x}{5} = 39$ _____   **16.** $\dfrac{x}{2} - \dfrac{5x}{6} = 7$ _____

17. $\dfrac{12x}{5} + \dfrac{4x}{2} = 22$ _____   **18.** $\dfrac{3x}{4} - \dfrac{5x}{12} = 5$ _____

19. $\dfrac{13x}{6} - \dfrac{5x}{7} = 122$ _____   **20.** $\dfrac{7x}{5} - \dfrac{4x}{9} = 43$ _____

21. $\dfrac{-20x}{3} + \dfrac{15x}{7} = 5$ _____   **22.** $\dfrac{-15x}{2} + \dfrac{11x}{5} = 106$ _____

23. $\dfrac{-5x}{21} + \dfrac{-3x}{7} = 7$ _____   **24.** $\dfrac{-3x}{17} + \dfrac{-2x}{34} = 4$ _____

25. $\dfrac{26x}{11} + \dfrac{7x}{2} = 129$ _____   **26.** $\dfrac{21x}{8} + \dfrac{9x}{3} = 81$ _____

Equations with Fractions

Name _____

Date _____ Period _____

Solve.

1. $\dfrac{x}{7} + \dfrac{x}{3} = 10$ $x = 21$ **2.** $\dfrac{x}{8} + \dfrac{x}{3} = 11$ _____

3. $\dfrac{x}{4} - \dfrac{x}{9} = 5$ _____   **4.** $\dfrac{x}{3} - \dfrac{x}{7} = 12$ _____

5. $\dfrac{x}{2} + \dfrac{x}{3} = -10$ _____   **6.** $\dfrac{x}{2} + \dfrac{x}{6} = -4$ _____

7. $\dfrac{x}{12} - \dfrac{x}{15} = 1$ _____   **8.** $\dfrac{x}{6} - \dfrac{x}{10} = 2$ _____

9. $\dfrac{x}{5} + \dfrac{x}{7} = 24$ _____   **10.** $\dfrac{2x}{9} - \dfrac{3x}{7} = 13$ _____

11. $\dfrac{4x}{5} + \dfrac{3x}{8} = 47$ _____   **12.** $\dfrac{2x}{3} - \dfrac{4x}{11} = 3$ _____

13. $\dfrac{3x}{7} + \dfrac{5x}{2} = 41$ _____   **14.** $\dfrac{3x}{5} + \dfrac{2x}{9} = 37$ _____

15. $\dfrac{-8x}{5} - \dfrac{x}{2} = 42$ _____   **16.** $\dfrac{4x}{3} - \dfrac{2x}{5} = 14$ _____

17. $\dfrac{x}{3} - \dfrac{2x}{7} = 2$ _____   **18.** $\dfrac{2x}{9} - \dfrac{3x}{7} = 26$ _____

19. $\dfrac{3x}{8} - \dfrac{5x}{12} = 1$ _____   **20.** $\dfrac{7x}{12} - \dfrac{4x}{15} = 19$ _____

21. $\dfrac{6x}{11} - \dfrac{8x}{9} = 17$ _____   **22.** $\dfrac{5x}{3} - \dfrac{9x}{5} = 2$ _____

23. $\dfrac{13x}{7} + \dfrac{5x}{3} = 8$ _____   **24.** $\dfrac{15x}{11} - \dfrac{13x}{7} = 1$ _____

25. $\dfrac{7x}{3} - \dfrac{2x}{5} = 2$ _____   **26.** $\dfrac{4x}{15} - \dfrac{5x}{12} = 1$ _____

Equations with Fractions

Solve.

1. $\dfrac{3x}{2} - \dfrac{3x}{8} = \dfrac{3}{4}$

$x = \dfrac{2}{3}$

2. $\dfrac{5x}{4} - \dfrac{3x}{8} = \dfrac{7}{12}$ _____

3. $\dfrac{4x}{3} + \dfrac{5x}{6} = \dfrac{13}{6}$ _____

4. $\dfrac{3x}{7} + \dfrac{5x}{14} = \dfrac{11}{14}$ _____

5. $\dfrac{3x}{5} - \dfrac{3x}{8} = \dfrac{9}{5}$ _____

6. $\dfrac{2x}{9} - \dfrac{5x}{12} = \dfrac{21}{4}$ _____

7. $\dfrac{5x}{12} - \dfrac{3x}{16} = 11$ _____

8. $\dfrac{7x}{6} - \dfrac{2x}{9} = 17$ _____

9. $\dfrac{7x}{20} - \dfrac{7x}{25} = \dfrac{7}{5}$ _____

10. $\dfrac{5x}{18} - \dfrac{5x}{24} = \dfrac{5}{4}$ _____

11. $\dfrac{3x}{8} + \dfrac{6x}{7} = \dfrac{23}{7}$ _____

12. $\dfrac{5x}{6} + \dfrac{5x}{8} = \dfrac{2}{3}$ _____

13. $\dfrac{3x}{5} - \dfrac{x}{3} = \dfrac{2}{5}$ _____

14. $\dfrac{x}{14} - \dfrac{3x}{21} = \dfrac{5}{7}$ _____

15. $\dfrac{2x}{3} - \dfrac{x}{6} = \dfrac{5}{4}$ _____

16. $\dfrac{6x}{11} - \dfrac{x}{2} = \dfrac{3}{4}$ _____

17. $\dfrac{5x}{6} - \dfrac{3x}{4} = \dfrac{1}{2}$ _____

18. $\dfrac{5x}{8} - \dfrac{3x}{4} = \dfrac{7}{8}$ _____

19. $\dfrac{11x}{8} - \dfrac{4x}{5} = \dfrac{9}{20}$ _____

20. $\dfrac{7x}{6} - \dfrac{3x}{4} = \dfrac{11}{12}$ _____

21. $\dfrac{11x}{12} + \dfrac{3x}{4} = \dfrac{5}{8}$ _____

22. $\dfrac{9x}{10} + \dfrac{7x}{20} = \dfrac{1}{5}$ _____

23. $\dfrac{5x}{6} - \dfrac{2x}{3} = \dfrac{3}{4}$ _____

24. $\dfrac{5x}{8} - \dfrac{2x}{5} = \dfrac{3}{10}$ _____

25. $\dfrac{15x}{7} + \dfrac{11x}{4} = \dfrac{137}{2}$ _____

26. $\dfrac{7x}{5} + \dfrac{x}{4} = \dfrac{9}{10}$ _____

Equations with Fractions

Name _____

Date _____ Period _____

_____

Solve.

1. $\dfrac{5x}{3} - \dfrac{7x}{12} = \dfrac{13}{6}$ $x = 2$

2. $\dfrac{3x}{5} - \dfrac{8x}{15} = \dfrac{1}{10}$ _____

3. $\dfrac{9x}{7} + \dfrac{11x}{14} = \dfrac{29}{21}$ _____

4. $\dfrac{7x}{6} + \dfrac{8x}{15} = \dfrac{3}{5}$ _____

5. $\dfrac{4x}{3} - \dfrac{3x}{2} = 3$ _____

6. $\dfrac{4x}{9} - \dfrac{7x}{15} = \dfrac{2}{3}$ _____

7. $\dfrac{-5x}{4} - \dfrac{-3x}{5} = 52$ _____

8. $\dfrac{-3x}{2} - \dfrac{-2x}{3} = 20$ _____

9. $\dfrac{5x}{14} - \dfrac{3x}{7} = \dfrac{8}{21}$ _____

10. $\dfrac{5x}{12} - \dfrac{3x}{16} = \dfrac{11}{24}$ _____

11. $\dfrac{3x}{5} - \dfrac{8x}{10} = \dfrac{7}{20}$ _____

12. $\dfrac{7x}{6} + \dfrac{11x}{15} = \dfrac{2}{3}$ _____

13. $\dfrac{5x}{11} + \dfrac{x}{2} = \dfrac{7}{22}$ _____

14. $\dfrac{13x}{8} - \dfrac{3x}{4} = \dfrac{5}{24}$ _____

15. $\dfrac{17x}{9} + \dfrac{19x}{12} = 5$ _____

16. $\dfrac{11x}{4} + \dfrac{7x}{12} = 20$ _____

17. $\dfrac{13x}{8} - \dfrac{7x}{12} = \dfrac{5}{8}$ _____

18. $\dfrac{5x}{9} - \dfrac{7x}{6} = \dfrac{11}{18}$ _____

19. $\dfrac{5x}{27} - \dfrac{11x}{9} = \dfrac{7}{3}$ _____

20. $\dfrac{8x}{15} + \dfrac{x}{5} = \dfrac{11}{10}$ _____

21. $\dfrac{4x}{7} + \dfrac{5x}{14} = \dfrac{13}{28}$ _____

22. $\dfrac{13x}{6} - \dfrac{7x}{4} = \dfrac{2}{3}$ _____

23. $\dfrac{13x}{15} - \dfrac{3x}{5} = \dfrac{3}{20}$ _____

24. $\dfrac{5x}{12} - \dfrac{x}{6} = \dfrac{5}{8}$ _____

25. $\dfrac{10x}{3} - \dfrac{7x}{5} = \dfrac{9}{10}$ _____

26. $\dfrac{9x}{4} - \dfrac{5x}{12} = \dfrac{7}{8}$ _____

         Developing Skills in Algebra   Book C

Equations with Fractions

Solve.

1. $\dfrac{x-3}{5} + 2 = \dfrac{x+4}{6}$ $x = -22$ **2.** $\dfrac{x+3}{5} - \dfrac{x-4}{7} = 21$

3. $\dfrac{x-4}{6} - \dfrac{x-1}{3} = \dfrac{1}{2}$ **4.** $\dfrac{x-2}{4} - \dfrac{x-1}{8} = \dfrac{1}{8}$

5. $\dfrac{x+5}{4} - \dfrac{x-3}{2} = -\dfrac{1}{2}$ **6.** $\dfrac{x+3}{6} - \dfrac{x-3}{10} = \dfrac{2}{15}$

7. $\dfrac{2x-3}{4} - \dfrac{3x+4}{5} = 1$ **8.** $\dfrac{3x-5}{6} + \dfrac{4x-8}{3} = 1$

9. $\dfrac{x-4}{8} + \dfrac{x+2}{3} = \dfrac{x+4}{4}$ **10.** $\dfrac{7x-1}{5} - \dfrac{5x+3}{6} = \dfrac{4x+3}{10}$

11. $\dfrac{8x-5}{12} - \dfrac{7x+3}{5} = \dfrac{x-4}{15}$ **12.** $\dfrac{9x-5}{6} - \dfrac{4-3x}{3} = \dfrac{20x+3}{9}$

13. $\dfrac{3x-4}{6} - \dfrac{5x-9}{9} = \dfrac{x-2}{3}$ **14.** $\dfrac{2x-1}{5} - \dfrac{4x+3}{10} = \dfrac{x-3}{2}$

15. $\dfrac{3x-1}{4} - \dfrac{5x+7}{8} = \dfrac{2x+3}{2}$ **16.** $\dfrac{2x+3}{3} - \dfrac{5x-2}{12} = \dfrac{3x-2}{6}$

17. $\dfrac{x+2}{7} - \dfrac{4x-5}{14} = \dfrac{3x+8}{2}$ **18.** $\dfrac{2x-7}{8} - \dfrac{3x-2}{4} = \dfrac{x-2}{10}$

19. $\dfrac{9x-4}{5} + \dfrac{x-3}{3} = \dfrac{2x+1}{15}$ **20.** $\dfrac{4x-3}{9} + \dfrac{3x+1}{3} = \dfrac{x-7}{12}$

21. $\dfrac{3x-2}{3} - \dfrac{2x-5}{4} = \dfrac{2x-4}{8}$ **22.** $\dfrac{2x-3}{2} - \dfrac{3x-3}{12} = \dfrac{7x+2}{6}$

23. $\dfrac{x+5}{4} - \dfrac{3x+7}{16} = \dfrac{5x-3}{12}$ **24.** $\dfrac{2x-5}{3} - \dfrac{5x-\frac{4}{3}}{5} = \dfrac{3x+5}{10}$

25. $\dfrac{x-1}{11} - \dfrac{3x+4}{2} = \dfrac{2x-2}{22}$ **26.** $\dfrac{3x+7}{9} - \dfrac{2x+1}{15} = \dfrac{x-2}{5}$

Name _____

Date _____ Period _____

Solve.

1. $\dfrac{4x}{9} + \dfrac{5x}{12} = \dfrac{2}{3}$ $x = \dfrac{24}{31}$

2. $\dfrac{8x}{9} + \dfrac{3x}{2} = \dfrac{5}{6}$

3. $\dfrac{x-9}{4} + 3 = \dfrac{x+2}{6}$

4. $\dfrac{x-3}{5} + 2 = \dfrac{x+1}{10}$

5. $\dfrac{x+3}{3} + \dfrac{x-4}{2} = \dfrac{1}{6}$

6. $\dfrac{x+2}{7} - \dfrac{x+3}{2} = \dfrac{3}{14}$

7. $\dfrac{2x-1}{4} - \dfrac{5x+2}{6} = 3$

8. $\dfrac{4x+1}{5} + \dfrac{3x+5}{3} = 2$

9. $\dfrac{x-5}{3} + \dfrac{x+4}{9} = \dfrac{x-2}{6}$

10. $\dfrac{6x-1}{7} - \dfrac{3x+2}{2} = \dfrac{2x+5}{14}$

11. $\dfrac{5x-4}{5} - \dfrac{2x+3}{3} = \dfrac{x+2}{6}$

12. $\dfrac{6x+3}{4} + \dfrac{2x+1}{3} = \dfrac{7x+2}{6}$

13. $\dfrac{2x-3}{5} - \dfrac{5x-2}{4} = \dfrac{x-1}{10}$

14. $\dfrac{3x+5}{2} - \dfrac{2x+5}{3} = \dfrac{x+2}{4}$

15. $\dfrac{5x+4}{3} - \dfrac{2x+7}{6} = \dfrac{4x+1}{9}$

16. $\dfrac{3x-1}{2} - \dfrac{7x+3}{10} = \dfrac{6x+11}{5}$

17. $\dfrac{x-6}{4} - \dfrac{3x-8}{12} = \dfrac{2x+1}{8}$

18. $\dfrac{x+1}{2} - \dfrac{2x+3}{7} = \dfrac{5x+2}{28}$

19. $\dfrac{4x-5}{8} - \dfrac{x+6}{3} = \dfrac{3x+7}{4}$

20. $\dfrac{5x-3}{5} - \dfrac{3x-2}{4} = \dfrac{x+7}{10}$

21. $\dfrac{x-3}{12} + \dfrac{2x-1}{15} = \dfrac{3x+1}{4}$

22. $\dfrac{5x-4}{10} + \dfrac{3x-3}{4} = \dfrac{9x-2}{12}$

23. $\dfrac{8x-5}{14} - \dfrac{x+11}{3} = \dfrac{7x}{6}$

24. $\dfrac{11x-3}{12} - \dfrac{5x}{3} = \dfrac{-(4x+3)}{5}$

25. $\dfrac{x-3}{5} + \dfrac{4x-5}{10} = \dfrac{8x-6}{15}$

26. $\dfrac{4x-2}{8} - \dfrac{5x-3}{4} = \dfrac{2x-1}{6}$

Developing Skills in Algebra   Book C

Equations with Fractions

Name _____

Date _____ Period _____

Solve.

1. $\frac{1}{3}\left(x - \frac{1}{2}\right) - \frac{1}{4}\left(x - \frac{1}{3}\right) = \frac{1}{3}$
$\underline{x = 5}$

2. $\frac{1}{3}(2x - 1) + \frac{1}{4}\left(\frac{1}{2} - 3x\right) = -2$
____

3. $\frac{1}{2}\left(2x - \frac{1}{2}\right) + \frac{3}{4}(x + 5) = \frac{7}{8}$
____

4. $\frac{4}{5}\left(3x - \frac{3}{4}\right) - \frac{1}{4}\left(2x - \frac{3}{5}\right) = \frac{1}{2}$
____

5. $\frac{1}{5}\left(x - \frac{5}{12}\right) - \frac{1}{6}\left(4x - \frac{3}{10}\right) = -\frac{4}{15}$
____

6. $\frac{4}{7}\left(6x - \frac{3}{5}\right) - \frac{3}{5}\left(5x - \frac{3}{7}\right) = \frac{6}{7}$
____

7. $\frac{1}{2}\left(\frac{2}{3} - \frac{1}{4}x\right) + \frac{1}{3}\left(\frac{3}{4} - \frac{1}{2}x\right) = \frac{1}{2}$
____

8. $\frac{1}{3}\left(\frac{1}{2} - \frac{x}{2}\right) - \frac{1}{2}\left(\frac{1}{2} + \frac{x}{3}\right) = -\frac{2}{9}$
____

9. $\frac{1}{2}(5x + 3) + \frac{5}{6}(2x - 1) = \frac{1}{4}(10x + 4)$
____

10. $\frac{1}{2}\left(8x - \frac{5}{11}\right) - \frac{10}{11}\left(5x + \frac{3}{8}\right) = -\frac{1}{4}(2x + 5)$
____

11. $\frac{2}{3}\left(2x + \frac{1}{2}\right) + \frac{14}{17}\left(\frac{13}{14} - 2x\right) = \frac{1}{3}(5 - x)$
____

12. $\frac{4}{9}\left(3x - \frac{1}{2}\right) - \frac{5}{7}\left(2x - \frac{8}{15}\right) = \frac{2}{3}\left(\frac{3}{8} - \frac{x}{7}\right)$
____

13. $\frac{3}{4}\left(17x + \frac{2}{9}\right) - \frac{5}{6}\left(15x + \frac{1}{5}\right) = \frac{1}{4}x$
____

14. $\frac{3}{5}\left(5x - \frac{1}{3}\right) - \frac{2}{3}\left(3x - \frac{3}{5}\right) = \frac{1}{2}(x + 2)$
____

15. $\frac{2}{5}\left(x - \frac{3}{2}\right) + \frac{1}{2}(x + 5) = \frac{1}{4}\left(x - \frac{1}{3}\right)$
____

16. $\frac{3}{8}\left(x - \frac{2}{3}\right) + \frac{1}{4}(x + 3) = \frac{1}{2}(x - 5)$
____

Name _____

Date _____ Period _____

Solve.

$x = -\frac{1}{6}$

1. $\frac{1}{4}\left(x + \frac{1}{4}\right) - \frac{1}{5}\left(x - \frac{1}{4}\right) = \frac{x+1}{8}$

2. $\frac{1}{5}(4x - 6) - \frac{1}{6}(3x - 1) = \frac{2}{15}x - \frac{1}{2}$ _____

3. $\frac{2}{3}\left(3x - \frac{1}{8}\right) - \frac{1}{4}\left(x - \frac{1}{2}\right) = \frac{3}{8}(2x + 5)$ _____

4. $\frac{7}{8}\left(6x - \frac{3}{7}\right) - \frac{4}{5}\left(5x + \frac{7}{16}\right) = \frac{9}{10}$ _____

5. $\frac{2}{3}\left(5x - \frac{1}{9}\right) + \frac{1}{3}\left(9x + \frac{4}{9}\right) = \frac{5}{27}$ _____

6. $\frac{8}{9}\left(8x - \frac{3}{8}\right) - \frac{3}{4}\left(9x + \frac{2}{3}\right) = \frac{5}{4}$ _____

7. $\frac{1}{2}(x - 3) + \left(x - \frac{1}{2}\right) = \frac{1}{3}(2x - 6)$ _____

8. $\frac{1}{5}\left(3 - \frac{x}{2}\right) - \frac{1}{8}\left(4 - \frac{x}{3}\right) = \frac{1}{10}\left(\frac{1-x}{6}\right)$ _____

9. $\frac{3}{8}\left(5x - \frac{2}{3}\right) + \frac{1}{6}\left(7x + \frac{1}{2}\right) = \frac{5}{16}\left(7x - \frac{2}{3}\right)$ _____

10. $\frac{4}{7}\left(5x - \frac{3}{16}\right) - \frac{5}{8}\left(4x - \frac{5}{7}\right) = \frac{1}{28}\left(9x + \frac{1}{2}\right)$ _____

11. $\frac{5}{12}\left(-7x - \frac{4}{5}\right) + \frac{5}{18}\left(10x + \frac{7}{10}\right) = -\frac{5}{9}\left(\frac{x}{5} - \frac{3}{4}\right)$ _____

12. $\frac{3}{25}\left(4x - \frac{2}{3}\right) - \frac{1}{5}\left(2x - \frac{3}{10}\right) = \frac{7}{10}\left(\frac{4x}{35} - \frac{2}{9}\right)$ _____

13. $\frac{3}{8}(24x + 11) - \frac{3}{4}(13x + 5) = -\frac{1}{16}(12x - 6)$ _____

14. $\frac{2}{5}\left(x - \frac{1}{3}\right) + \frac{1}{2}(x + 2) = \frac{7}{10}\left(x - \frac{4}{7}\right)$ _____

15. $\frac{5}{9}\left(x + \frac{3}{5}\right) + \frac{1}{6}(x - 4) = \frac{2}{3}(x + 1)$ _____

16. $\frac{2}{3}\left(x - \frac{1}{2}\right) + \frac{3}{4}\left(x + \frac{2}{3}\right) = \frac{5}{6}\left(x - \frac{1}{5}\right)$ _____

 Developing Skills in Algebra   Book C

Equations with Fractions

Name _____

Date _____ Period _____

Solve.

1. $0.4x - 0.15x = 7.5$ ⟶ *x* = 30

2. $0.81x + 0.07x = 1.1$ _____

3. $1.23x - 0.03x = 14.4$ _____

4. $0.75x - 0.31 = -0.8x$ _____

5. $1.08x - 80 = 0.92x$ _____

6. $3.4x + 9.4 = 1.05x$ _____

7. $4.4x + 0.03(14x - 0.7) = 16.849$ _____

8. $2.4x - 0.07(4x - 0.3) = 1.505$ _____

9. $3.9x + 0.6(3.4x - 0.8) = 13.182$ _____

10. $7.1x - 5.077 = 0.42(6x - 5)$ _____

11. $11.1x - 1.725 = -0.51(3x - 9)$ _____

12. $5.4x - 1.745 = 0.2(0.7x + 11)$ _____

13. $0.42(x + 3) - 0.81(2x - 5) + 0.76 = 26.47$ _____

14. $0.27(5x - 2) + 0.55(4x + 7) - 1.2 = 179.61$ _____

15. $0.64(3x - 7) - 0.21(2x + 9) - 4.3 = 37.33$ _____

16. $0.05(x - 0.1) + 0.03(2x - 2) = 0.4(3x + 0.11)$ _____

Equations with Fractions

Name _____

Date _____ Period _____

Solve.

1. $0.8x - 0.05x = 0.3$ *x = 0.4*

2. $0.12x + 7.8x = 1.8216$ _____

3. $1.45x - 0.05x = 28$ _____

4. $0.65x - 0.27 = -0.7x$ _____

5. $1.12x - 13 = 0.86x$ _____

6. $6.12x + 80.8 = 2.08x$ _____

7. $3.5x + 0.04(11x - 0.6) = 17.706$ _____

8. $6.7x - 0.09(8x - 0.5) = 10.211$ _____

9. $7.4x + 0.5(6.2x - 0.7) = 65.275$ _____

10. $9.3x - 8.331 = 0.63(4x - 3)$ _____

11. $12.3x - 6.716 = -0.83(7x - 5)$ _____

12. $2.3x + 3.319 = 0.4(0.8x + 13)$ _____

13. $0.36(2x - 5) - 0.76(3x + 2) + 0.83 = 30.27$ _____

14. $0.35(4x - 3) + 0.75(9x - 5) - 2.1 = 188.7$ _____

15. $0.98(2x - 1) - 0.19(4x + 13) + 1.8 = 21.15$ _____

16. $0.01(x - 0.9) + 0.04(3x - 23) = 0.5(4x + 0.012)$ _____

Fractional Equations

Name _____

Date _____ Period _____

Solve.

1. $\dfrac{x-2}{x+1} + \dfrac{x-3}{x-1} = 2$ $x = \frac{1}{5}$

2. $\dfrac{x-3}{x+4} + \dfrac{2x+1}{x-4} = 3$

3. $\dfrac{x}{x+4} + \dfrac{2x-6}{x-3} = 3$

4. $\dfrac{x+4}{x-3} - \dfrac{2x-5}{x-2} = -1$

5. $\dfrac{3x}{6-2x} + \dfrac{5x+4}{2x+7} = 1$

6. $\dfrac{2x}{4-2x} + \dfrac{3x+2}{x+4} = 2$

7. $\dfrac{y+6}{y-3} - \dfrac{2y-4}{y-5} = -1$

8. $\dfrac{x-5}{x-2} - \dfrac{3x-2}{x+1} = -2$

9. $\dfrac{1}{y^2} - \dfrac{5}{y-1} = \dfrac{-5}{y}$

10. $\dfrac{2}{x^2} - \dfrac{6}{x-2} = \dfrac{-6}{x}$

11. $\dfrac{x+2}{x+3} + \dfrac{2x+5}{x-2} = 3$

12. $\dfrac{x-2}{x+4} + \dfrac{3x+2}{x-1} = 4$

13. $\dfrac{x-1}{x+5} + \dfrac{x+2}{x+3} = 2$

14. $\dfrac{x-2}{x+3} + \dfrac{3x+1}{x-2} = 4$

15. $\dfrac{4x}{x-1} + \dfrac{3x}{x+1} = 7$

16. $\dfrac{3x}{x-2} + \dfrac{2x}{x+2} = 5$

17. $\dfrac{x-1}{x+3} + \dfrac{x+2}{x-3} = 2$

18. $\dfrac{x-2}{x+4} + \dfrac{x+3}{x-2} = 2$

19. $\dfrac{2x+5}{x+3} - \dfrac{4x+1}{x-2} = -2$

20. $\dfrac{3x+1}{x-2} - \dfrac{5x+1}{x-1} = -2$

21. $\dfrac{x+2}{x-3} + \dfrac{x-1}{x-2} = 2$

22. $\dfrac{x+3}{x-2} + \dfrac{5x+1}{x-3} = 6$

23. $\dfrac{2x-3}{x} + \dfrac{5x-3}{x^2} - \dfrac{2x^2+x-6}{x^3} = 2$

24. $\dfrac{2x-1}{x} + \dfrac{3x-2}{x^2} - \dfrac{5x^2-x+3}{x^3} = 2\left(1 - \dfrac{3}{2x}\right)$

Developing Skills in Algebra   Book C

Fractional Equations

Name _____

Date _____ Period _____

Solve.

1. $\dfrac{x+1}{x+2} - \dfrac{x-1}{x-2} = \dfrac{x-9}{x+2}$ $x = 3 \text{ or } 6$

2. $\dfrac{x+3}{x-1} + \dfrac{1-3x}{x+1} = \dfrac{2}{x^2-1}$

3. $\dfrac{2x+2}{x-1} + \dfrac{2x-7}{x+3} = \dfrac{7x+2}{3x-3}$

4. $\dfrac{x+7}{2x+2} - \dfrac{x+2}{x+1} = \dfrac{-3x+3}{5x-5}$

5. $\dfrac{3-x}{2x} + \dfrac{x+1}{x-1} = \dfrac{9x+1}{4x}$

6. $\dfrac{x-4}{x-1} + \dfrac{x-3}{x+6} = \dfrac{2x-3}{x+6}$

7. $\dfrac{x+1}{3x+2} + \dfrac{2x-1}{x+2} = \dfrac{4x+1}{3x+2}$

8. $\dfrac{2x-1}{2x} - \dfrac{x}{x+1} = \dfrac{x-2}{4x}$

9. $\dfrac{x}{x+1} - \dfrac{x-1}{2x+2} = \dfrac{x+1}{2x+2}$

10. $\dfrac{x-5}{2x-1} - \dfrac{x-4}{x-3} = \dfrac{-(x+1)}{2x-1}$

11. $\dfrac{3x}{3x+1} - \dfrac{x}{11x+1} = \dfrac{5x+3}{11x+1}$

12. $\dfrac{x-2}{x+2} + \dfrac{x-1}{2x+4} = \dfrac{2x-1}{2x+4}$

13. $\dfrac{x-2}{x-1} + \dfrac{1}{x-7} = \dfrac{x+1}{x-7}$

14. $\dfrac{x+3}{x-11} + \dfrac{x-8}{x-3} = \dfrac{4x+1}{x-3}$

15. $\dfrac{x+2}{2x-2} - \dfrac{x-2}{x-1} = \dfrac{6-x}{2x-2}$

16. $\dfrac{4x}{4x+2} - \dfrac{x-1}{2x+1} = \dfrac{2x+2}{4x+2}$

17. $\dfrac{4x+1}{8x+2} + \dfrac{x+2}{4x+1} = \dfrac{x}{8x+2}$

18. $\dfrac{2x+2}{3x} + \dfrac{x-3}{2x-5} = \dfrac{x+1}{3x}$

19. $\dfrac{x+4}{2x+4} - \dfrac{x-3}{x+2} = \dfrac{x-2}{2x+4}$

20. $\dfrac{x-1}{x+4} - \dfrac{x-9}{2x+8} = \dfrac{x+5}{2x+8}$

21. $\dfrac{x}{x+1} + \dfrac{x-3}{2x+2} = \dfrac{3x-3}{2x+2}$

22. $\dfrac{x+1}{x+2} + \dfrac{x-4}{x-3} = \dfrac{2x+1}{x+2}$

23. $\dfrac{3x+1}{6x} - \dfrac{x-1}{5x-4} = \dfrac{2x+1}{6x}$

24. $\dfrac{3x-1}{2x+3} - \dfrac{x-1}{2x-3} = \dfrac{x-1}{2x+3}$

     Developing Skills in Algebra   Book C

Fractional Equations

Name _____

Date _____ Period _____

Solve.

1. $\dfrac{x}{x-1} - \dfrac{x+1}{x+2} = \dfrac{x-1}{x+2}$ $x = 0 \text{ or } 4$

2. $\dfrac{x-6}{x-1} + \dfrac{x-4}{x+7} = \dfrac{x+2}{x+7}$

3. $\dfrac{x-10}{x-9} + \dfrac{x-3}{x+1} = \dfrac{x+9}{x+1}$

4. $\dfrac{x-2}{x-1} - \dfrac{2x-7}{2x+4} = \dfrac{x+1}{2x+4}$

5. $\dfrac{x-9}{x-7} + \dfrac{x-10}{x+9} = \dfrac{2x-7}{x+9}$

6. $\dfrac{x-15}{x-3} + \dfrac{x}{x+12} = \dfrac{x+6}{x+12}$

7. $\dfrac{x+4}{2x-4} - \dfrac{x-5}{3x+2} = \dfrac{2x+3}{3x+2}$

8. $\dfrac{x+8}{2x+1} - \dfrac{3x-4}{4x+2} = \dfrac{x-4}{4x+2}$

9. $\dfrac{x+8}{x+10} + \dfrac{x-13}{x-5} = \dfrac{2x+2}{x+10}$

10. $\dfrac{x+1}{2x+2} + \dfrac{x-1}{2x+2} = \dfrac{x}{x+1}$

11. $\dfrac{x+3}{3x+2} + \dfrac{x+1}{3x+2} = \dfrac{x+2}{x+3}$

12. $\dfrac{x-1}{x+6} - \dfrac{x-6}{3x+1} = \dfrac{x+4}{3x+1}$

13. $\dfrac{2x}{4x+4} - \dfrac{x-1}{2x+2} = \dfrac{x-3}{2x+2}$

14. $\dfrac{2x+5}{5x} + \dfrac{x-6}{2x-10} = \dfrac{4x+5}{5x}$

15. $\dfrac{2x+1}{2x} + \dfrac{x-4}{2x-7} = \dfrac{4x-7}{2x}$

16. $\dfrac{2x+2}{3x-1} + \dfrac{x-2}{5x+3} = \dfrac{5x+2}{5x+3}$

17. $\dfrac{x}{4x+2} - \dfrac{x+1}{x+3} = \dfrac{-(2x+3)}{4x+2}$

18. $\dfrac{x+5}{2x-1} - \dfrac{5x+4}{6x-3} = \dfrac{x-13}{6x-3}$

19. $\dfrac{3x+2}{7x-2} + \dfrac{x-3}{x+4} = \dfrac{5x+2}{7x-2}$

20. $\dfrac{x+1}{8x-1} + \dfrac{x}{2x+1} = \dfrac{4x+1}{8x-1}$

21. $\dfrac{x-11}{2x-8} + \dfrac{x-5}{x-4} = \dfrac{x+11}{2x-8}$

22. $\dfrac{x+1}{2x-3} - \dfrac{1}{2x-3} = 1$

23. $\dfrac{3x+3}{2x-6} - \dfrac{x+5}{2x-6} = \dfrac{x-1}{x-3}$

24. $\dfrac{4x+4}{2x} - \dfrac{3x+7}{2x} = \dfrac{x-5}{2x-7}$

25

Fractional Equations

Solve.

1. $x + \dfrac{-1}{x} = 0$ $x = \pm 1$

2. $x + \dfrac{28}{x} = 11$

3. $\dfrac{x}{x + 1} = \dfrac{2x}{x - 1}$

4. $\dfrac{2x^2 + 4}{x} = \dfrac{4}{x} - 3$

5. $\dfrac{x^2 + 2x + 1}{x^2 - 4x + 4} = \dfrac{1}{4}$

6. $\dfrac{2x + 3}{3x + 2} = \dfrac{6x + 6}{5x + 4}$

7. $\dfrac{1}{x} + \dfrac{1}{x + 1} = \dfrac{x^2 - 2}{x^2 + x}$

8. $\dfrac{2x + 1}{3x + 1} + \dfrac{x - 1}{2x - 1} = \dfrac{4x - 1}{3x + 1}$

9. $\dfrac{x + 1}{2x - 4} - \dfrac{2x - 1}{3x} = \dfrac{3x - 4}{3x}$

10. $\dfrac{x^2 - 5x + 6}{x^2 + 7x + 12} = \dfrac{x - 3}{x + 3}$

11. $\dfrac{3x + 1}{x + 1} - \dfrac{2x + 2}{x - 2} = \dfrac{x + 3}{x + 1}$

12. $\dfrac{2x}{x - 3} + \dfrac{x + 1}{x - 5} = \dfrac{4x + 2}{x - 3}$

13. $\dfrac{x + 1}{x - 5} + \dfrac{x + 4}{x - 7} = \dfrac{2x - 1}{x - 7}$

14. $\dfrac{6 - x - x^2}{x^2} + \dfrac{9 + 4x}{x} - \dfrac{8x^2 - 1}{x^3} = 3$

15. $\dfrac{4}{x - 2} - \dfrac{5}{x + 2} = \dfrac{20}{x^2 - 4}$

16. $\dfrac{12}{3x - 2} - \dfrac{8}{3x + 2} + \dfrac{33x - 2}{4 - 9x^2} = 0$

17. $\dfrac{3}{x - 1} - \dfrac{4x - 1}{x + 1} = \dfrac{x^2 + 5}{x^2 - 1} - 5$

18. $\dfrac{x + 3}{x + 2} + \dfrac{x - 3}{x - 2} = \dfrac{x^2 + 4}{x^2 - 4}$

19. $\dfrac{x + 2}{x - 2} + \dfrac{x + 3}{x - 3} = \dfrac{2}{x^2 - 5x + 6}$

20. $\dfrac{7}{x - 2} + \dfrac{3}{x - 10} = \dfrac{2x + 10}{x^2 - 12x + 20}$

21. $\dfrac{10x + 1}{2(x + 1)} - \dfrac{8x^2 + 6x - 8}{4(x + 1)^2} = 3$

22. $\dfrac{x + 1}{2x - 3} - \dfrac{x - 1}{2x^2 - 5x + 3} = 1$

26

Investment Problems   Name _____

Date _____ Period _____

Show a complete solution for each problem.

1. Two sums of money were invested at 13% and 15%, respectively. The amount invested at 15% was twice the amount invested at 13%. The total annual income from the two investments was $227.90. How much was invested at each rate? $0.13m + 0.15(2m) = 227.90$

   m = am't. at 13%

   $2m$ = am't. at 15%

   $0.43m = 227.90$

   $m = 530$

   The 13% investment was $530 and the 15% investment was $1060.

2. Two sums of money were invested at 12% and 8.5%, respectively. The amount invested at 12% was three times the amount invested at 8.5%. The total annual income from the two investments was $151.30. How much was invested at each rate?

3. Jim borrowed some money at 13% interest and some money at 16% interest. The amount at 16% was $200 more than twice the amount borrowed at 13%. How much was borrowed at each rate if he had to pay a total of $234.50 annual interest?

4. The money that Ann borrowed at 19% interest was $500 less than three times the amount she borrowed at 13%. How much did she borrow at each rate if she had to pay a total of $412.50 annual interest?

5. In a savings account at Ace Savings, Julie had some money that earned 6.5% interest. She had $400 more than that amount in a savings account at Busby Federal. The amount in Busby's earned 7.5% interest. How much was invested in each account if her income from the two accounts was $130.80?

6. In a savings account at Alum Savings and Loan, Ralph had money that earned 8.5% interest. He had money in a savings account at Barnum & Bailey Bank that earned 9.6% interest. He had $820 more in the account at Barnum & Bailey than in the account at Alum. His annual income from the two accounts was $158.36. How much did he have in each account?

7. Mr. Toya had part of his $4000 savings in an account that earned 7% interest and the rest in an account that earned 9% interest. How much did he have in each account if his annual income from the total investment was $404.20?

8. Mrs. Able had savings of $7000, part of which was invested at 12% interest and the rest at 10% interest. How much did she have invested at each rate if her annual income from the investments was $761?

Investment Problems

Name _____

Date _____ Period _____

Show a complete solution for each problem.

1. Two sums of money were invested at 12% and 18%, respectively. The amount invested at 18% was twice the amount invested at 12%. The total annual income from the two investments was $1310.40. How much was invested at each rate?

$m = am't.\ at\ 12\%$
$2m = am't.\ at\ 18\%$

$0.12m + 0.18(2m) = 1310.40$
$0.48m = 1310.40$
$m = 2730$

The 12% investment was $2730. The 18% investment was $5460.

2. Two sums of money were invested at 8% and 11%, respectively. The amount invested at 11% was three times the amount invested at 8%. The total annual income from the two investments was $721.60. How much was invested at each rate?

3. Tom borrowed some money at 13% interest and some money at 15% interest. The amount at 13% was $230 more than twice the amount borrowed at 15%. How much was borrowed at each rate if he had to pay a total of $242.69 annual interest?

4. The money that Tia borrowed at 14% interest was $500 less than three times the amount she borrowed at 12%. How much did she borrow at each rate if she had to pay a total of $418.16 annual interest?

5. In a savings account at Coast Federal, Anne had some money that earned 7.3% interest. She had $300 more than that amount in a savings account at Rock Bottom Bank. The amount in the Rock Bottom account earned 8.1% interest. How much was invested in each account if her income from the two accounts was $132.10?

6. In a savings account at Safety First Federal, Harold had money that earned 6.3% interest. He had money in a savings account at Home Savings that earned 7.8% interest. He had $710 more in the account at Home Savings than in his account at Safety First. His annual income from the two accounts was $166.77. How much did he have in each account?

7. Mr. Hill had part of his $5000 savings in an account that earned 8% interest and the rest in an account that earned 12% interest. How much did he have in each account if his annual income from the total investment was $514.80?

8. Mrs. Pine had savings of $9000, part of which was invested at 7% interest and the rest at 9% interest. How much did she have invested at each rate if her annual income from the investments was $741.60?

Mixture Problems

Name _____

Date _____ Period _____

Show a complete solution for each problem.

1. Candy worth $1.65 a pound was mixed with candy worth $1.23 a pound. How many pounds of each were used if there was twice as much of the $1.23 candy as there was of the $1.65 candy and if the value of the mixture was $20.55?

c = am't. $1.65 candy $1.65c + 1.23(2c) = 20.55$ *There were 5 pounds of $1.65 candy and 10 pounds of $1.23 candy.*
$2c$ = am't. $1.23 candy $4.11c = 20.55$
                                  $c = 5$

2. Candy worth $2.75 a pound was mixed with candy worth $1.50 a pound. How many pounds of each were used if there was three times as much of the $1.50 candy as there was of the $2.75 candy and if the value of the mixture was $50.75?

3. Peanuts worth $2.50 a pound were mixed with cashews worth $3.25 a pound. How many pounds of each were used if there were ten more pounds of peanuts than cashews and if the value of the mixture was $122.75?

4. Almonds worth $3.95 a pound were mixed with walnuts worth $4.25 a pound. How many pounds of each were used if there were 15 more pounds of almonds than walnuts and if the value of the mixture was $239.65?

5. Two kinds of coffee were blended together, one worth $6.50 a pound and the other worth $5.95 a pound. The blend contained ten pounds more than twice as much of the $5.95 coffee than of the $6.50 coffee. How much of each kind was used if the value of the blend is $280.30?

6. A blend of coffee was made by using coffee worth $4.25 a pound and coffee worth $3.49 a pound. The blend contained seven pounds less than three times as much of the $3.49 coffee than of the $4.25 coffee. How much of each kind was used if the total value of the blend was $196.37?

7. Twenty pounds of dried fruit mix contained prunes worth $2.90 a pound and apricots worth $3.15 a pound. How many pounds of each did the mix contain if the total value of the mix was $59.75?

8. Thirty pounds of dried fruit mix contained apples worth $2.75 a pound and pears worth $3.85 a pound. How many pounds of each did the mix contain if the value of the mix was $96.80?

                    Developing Skills in Algebra   Book C

Mixture Problems

Show a complete solution for each problem.

1. Candy worth $1.85 a pound was mixed with candy worth $2.34 a pound. How many pounds of each were used if there was twice as much $2.34 candy as the $1.85 candy and if the value of the mixture was $78.36?

$1.85c + 2.34(2c) = 78.36$

$c = $ am't. $1.85 candy
$2c = $ am't. $2.34 candy

$6.53c = 78.36$
$c = 12$

There were 12 lbs of $1.85 candy and 24 lbs of $2.34 candy.

2. Candy worth $3.25 a pound was mixed with candy worth $2.70 a pound. How many pounds of each were used if there was three times as much of the $2.70 candy as the $3.25 candy and if the value of the mixture was $90.80?

3. Peanuts worth $3.60 a pound were mixed with cashews worth $4.25 a pound. How many pounds of each were used if there were 7 more pounds of cashews than peanuts and if the value of the mixture was $131.80?

4. Almonds worth $4.95 a pound were mixed with walnuts worth $3.95 a pound. How many pounds of each were used if there were 11 more pounds of almonds than walnuts and if the value of the mixture was $116.75?

5. Two kinds of coffee were blended together, one worth $5.40 a pound and the other worth $6.25 a pound. The blend contained ten pounds more than twice as much of the $5.40 coffee than of the $6.25 coffee. How much of each kind was used if the value of the blend was $190.40?

6. A blend of coffee was made by using coffee worth $5.85 a pound and coffee worth $4.50 a pound. The blend contained seven pounds less than twice as much of the $4.50 coffee than of the $5.85 coffee. How much of each kind was used if the total value of the blend was $310.05?

7. Twenty pounds of dried fruit mix contained prunes worth $3.50 a pound and apricots worth $2.95 a pound. How many pounds of each did the mix contain if the total value of the mix was $66.15?

8. Thirty pounds of dried fruit mix contained apples worth $3.15 a pound and pears worth $4.25 a pound. How many pounds of each did the mix contain if the value of the mix was $107.70?

Name _____

Date _____ Period _____

Show a complete solution for each problem.

1. How many kilograms of zinc that is 18% pure should be mixed with 16 kilograms of alloy that is 24% pure to make an alloy that is 22% pure zinc?

z = am't 18% zinc $0.18z + 0.24(16) = 0.22(z+16)$ *You need 8 kg of*
$z+16$ = am't 22% zinc $0.18z + 3.84 = 0.22z + 3.52$ *zinc that is 18% pure.*
                                $0.04z = 0.32$
                                $z = 8$

2. Thirty-three kilograms of nickel that was 35% pure were mixed with a nickel alloy that was 21% pure. How many kilograms of each kind were used to produce an alloy that was 27% pure?

3. Copper that was 95% pure was melted together with copper that was 75% pure to make 15 kilograms of an alloy that was 83% pure. How many kilograms of each kind were used?

4. Tin that was 35% pure was melted together with tin that was 45% pure to make 20 kilograms of an alloy that was 39% pure. How many kilograms of each were used?

5. Milk with 3% butterfat was mixed with cream with 27% butterfat to produce 36 L of half-and-half with 11% butterfat content. How much of each was used?

6. A 45% salt solution was mixed with a 75% salt solution to produce 15 kilograms of solution that was 67% salt. How much of each solution was used?

7. How much water was added to 3 L of a 27% boric acid solution to produce a solution that was 18% boric acid?

8. How much water was evaporated from 8 L of a 25% salt solution to produce a solution that was 40% salt?

9. A radiator contains 6 L of a 48% antifreeze mixture. How much pure antifreeze should be added to make a mixture that is 74% antifreeze?

10. A small vat contains 48 L of a 5% sulphuric acid solution. How much pure sulphuric acid should be added to make a solution that is 24% pure?

Mixture Problems

Name _____

Date _____ Period _____

Show a complete solution for each problem.

1. How many kilograms of zinc that is 33% pure should be mixed with 12 kilograms of alloy that is 45% pure to make an alloy that is 39% pure zinc?

z = am't. 33% zinc $0.33z + 0.45(12) = 0.39(z+12)$ You need 12 kg
$z+12$ = am't. 39% zinc $0.33z + 5.4 = 0.39z + 4.68$ of 33% zinc.
                            $0.72 = 0.06z$
                               $12 = z$

2. Thirty kilograms of nickel that was 38% pure were mixed with a nickel alloy that was 28% pure. How many kilograms of each kind were used to produce an alloy that was 32% pure?

3. Copper that was 63% pure was melted together with copper that was 90% pure to make 18 kilograms of an alloy that was 75% pure. How many kilograms of each kind were used?

4. Tin that was 48% pure was melted together with tin that was 44% pure to make 20 kilograms of an alloy that was 45% pure. How many kilograms of each were used?

5. Milk with 3% butterfat was mixed with cream with 36% butterfat to produce 33 L of half-and-half with 18% butterfat content. How much of each was used?

6. A 56% salt solution was mixed with a 42% salt solution to produce 21 kilograms of solution that was 48% salt. How much of each solution was used?

7. How much water was added to 12 L of a 35% boric acid solution to produce a solution that was 20% boric acid?

8. How much water was evaporated from 7 L of a 52% salt solution to produce a solution that was 91% salt?

9. A radiator contains 6 L of a 44% antifreeze mixture. How much pure antifreeze should be added to make a mixture that is 52% antifreeze?

10. A small vat contains 26 L of a 5% sulphuric acid solution. How much pure sulphuric acid should be added to make a solution that is 35% pure?

          Developing Skills in Algebra   Book C

Motion Problems

Name _____

Date _____ Period _____

Show a complete solution for each problem.

1. A freight train made two 180 km trips. It made the second trip in 3 hours less time by increasing the rate of travel by 10 km/h. Find each rate at which the train traveled.

$r = $ rate of first trip
$r + 10 = $ rate of second trip

$\dfrac{180}{r} - 3 = \dfrac{180}{r+10}$

$\dfrac{180 - 3r}{r} = \dfrac{180}{r+10}$

$\Big\} \Rightarrow 1800 + 150r - 3r^2 = 180r$
$3r^2 + 30r - 1800 = 0$
$r = 20$

The rates are 20 km/h and 30 km/h.

2. Mr. Harris drove 360 km round trip. On the return trip, he increased his average rate of travel by 9 km/h and made the trip in 2 hours less time. Find his rate of travel for each direction.

3. Mr. Lyle made a round trip between two cities that were 450 km apart. On the return trip, he increased his average rate of travel by 5 km/h and made the trip in 1 hour less time. Find his rate of travel for each direction.

4. Mrs. Lawson traveled between two cities that were 840 km apart. On the return trip, she increased her average rate of travel by 16 km/h and made the trip in 6 hours less time. Find the rate of travel for each direction.

5. Mr. Smith traveled 1152 km by automobile and returned two weeks later. His average rate of travel on the return trip was 16 km/h less than it was going, and the trip back took 6 hours longer. Find the time he spent traveling in each direction.

6. On a round trip of 700 km in each direction, Mr. Anderson averaged 7 km/h more returning than he did going. If the return trip took 5 hours less than the trip going, find the time he spent traveling in each direction.

7. Mr. Donley drove 720 km in each direction on a vacation trip. The average rate going was 12 km/h more than the rate returning. The total time for the entire trip was 35 hours. Find the average rate for each direction.

8. On a round trip of 504 km in each direction, the total trip took 21 hours. The average rate of travel was 14 km/h less on the return trip. Find the rate for each direction.

9. After driving for 220 km, Harry increased his average rate of travel by 5 km/h and traveled 300 km more. Find each rate if the total trip took 10 hours.

10. After driving for 216 km, Mr. Orosco increased his rate of travel by 3 km/h and traveled 360 km more. The total time for the trip was 20 hours. Find the rate for each part of the trip.

Motion Problems

Name _____

Date _____ Period _____

Show a complete solution for each problem.

1. A freight train made two 336 km trips. It made the second trip in 1 hour less time by increasing its rate of travel by 6 km/h. Find each rate at which the train traveled.

$r = $ rate of first trip

$r + 6 = $ rate of second trip

$\frac{336}{r} - 1 = \frac{336}{r+6}$

$\frac{336 - r}{r} = \frac{336}{r+6}$

$2016 + 330r - r^2 = 336r$

$r^2 + 6r - 2016 = 0$

$r = 42$ or 48

The rates are 42 km/h and 48 km/h.

2. Mr. Halley made two 468 km trips. He made the second trip in 3 hours less time by increasing his average rate of travel by 26 km/h. Find each rate at which he traveled.

3. Mr. Lewis made a round trip between two cities that were 200 km apart. On the return trip, he increased the average rate of travel by 5 km/h and made the trip in 2 hours less time. Find his rate of travel for each direction.

4. Mrs. Kness traveled between two cities that were 420 km apart. On the return trip, she increased her average rate of travel by 7 km/h and made the trip in 3 hours less time. Find the rate of travel in each direction.

5. Bill traveled 468 km by automobile and returned two weeks later. His average rate of travel on the return trip was 26 km/h more than it was going, and the trip back took 3 hours less time. Find the time he spent traveling in each direction.

6. On a round trip of 540 km in each direction, Mr. Armstrong averaged 9 km/h more returning than he did going. If the return trip took 2 hours less than the trip going, find the time for each direction.

7. Mr. Levi drove 1200 km in each direction on a vacation trip. The average rate going was 5 km/h more than the rate returning. The total time for the entire trip was 24 hours. Find the average rate for each direction.

8. On a round trip of 252 km in each direction, the average rate of travel was 7 km/h more than the rate returning. Find the rate for each direction if the entire trip took 21 hours.

9. After driving for 240 km, Larry decreased his average rate of travel by 3 km/h and traveled 450 km more. Find each rate if the total trip took 15 hours.

10. After driving for 360 km, Mr. Mackey decreased his rate of travel by 5 km/h and traveled 200 km more. The total time for the trip was 20 hours. Find the rate for each part of the trip.

Name _____

Date _____ Period _____

Show a complete solution for each problem.

1. A freight train made two 200 km trips. It made the second trip in 1 hour less time by increasing the rate of travel by 10 km/h. Find each rate at which the train traveled. *The rates are*

   $r = \text{rate of first trip}$ $\dfrac{200}{r} - 1 = \dfrac{200}{r+10}$ $2000 + 1900 - r^2 = 200r$ *40 km/h and*

   $r + 10 = \text{rate of second trip}$ $\dfrac{200 - r}{r} = \dfrac{200}{r+10}$ $r^2 + 10r - 2000 = 0$ *50 km/h.*

   $r = 40 \text{ or } 50$

2. Mr. Lopez made two 330 km trips. He made the second trip in 1 hour less time by increasing his average rate of travel by 3 km/h. Find each rate at which he traveled.

3. Mr. Jones made a round trip between two cities that were 200 km apart. On the return trip, he increased his average rate of travel by 10 km/h and made the trip in 1 hour less time. Find his rate of travel for each direction.

4. Mrs. Watt traveled between two cities that were 750 km apart. On the return trip, she increased her average rate of travel by 20 km/h and made the trip in 10 hours less time. Find her rate of travel in each direction.

5. Walt traveled 360 km by automobile and returned two weeks later. His average rate of travel on the return trip was 10 km/h more than it was going, and the trip took 6 hours less time. Find the time he spent traveling in each direction.

6. On a round trip of 480 km in each direction, Mr. Watson averaged 10 km/h more returning than he did going. If the return trip took 4 hours less, find his time for each direction.

7. Mr. Ing drove 600 km in each direction on a vacation trip. The average rate going was 20 km/h more than the rate returning. The total time for the entire trip was 32 hours. Find the average rate for each direction.

8. On a round trip of 540 km in each direction, the average rate of travel going was 30 km/h more than the rate returning. Find the rate for each direction if the entire trip took 15 hours.

9. After driving for 330 km, Mary decreased her average rate of travel by 11 km/h and traveled 440 km more. Find each rate if the total trip took 13 hours.

10. After driving for 168 km, Margaret decreased her rate of travel by 7 km/h and traveled 105 km more. The total time for the trip was 7 hours. Find the rate for each part of the trip.

Motion Problems

Name _____

Date _____ Period _____

Show a complete solution for each problem.

1. A freight train made two 150 km trips. It made the second trip in 1 hour less time by increasing the rate of travel by 5 km/h. Find each rate at which the train traveled.

r = rate of first trip $\qquad \frac{150}{r} - 1 = \frac{150}{r+5}$ → $750 + 145r - r^2 = 150r$ 　The rates are
$r + 5$ = rate of second trip $\qquad \frac{150-r}{r} = \frac{150}{r+5}$ 　$r^2 + 5r - 750 = 0$ 　20 km/h and
$\qquad\qquad r = 20$ 　25 km/h.

2. Mr. Bark made two 252 km trips. He made the second trip in 1 hour less time by increasing his average rate of travel by 6 km/h. Find each rate at which he traveled.

3. Mr. Wu traveled 126 km by bicycle and returned the same way. On the return trip, he increased his average rate of travel by 7 km/h and made the trip in 3 hours less time. Find his rate of travel for each direction.

4. Mrs. Wilson traveled between two cities that were 330 km apart. On the return trip, she increased her average rate of travel by 25 km/h and made the trip in 5 hours less time. Find her rate of travel in each direction.

5. John traveled 252 km by automobile and returned two weeks later. His average rate of travel on the return trip was 14 km/h more than it was going, and the trip took 3 hours less time. Find the time he spent traveling in each direction.

6. On a round trip of 350 km in each direction, Mr. Sinclair averaged 10 km/h more returning than he did going. If the return trip took 4 hours less time, find the time for each direction.

7. Mr. Hope drove 420 km in each direction on a vacation trip. The average rate going was 24 km/h more than the rate returning. The total time for the entire trip was 12 hours. Find his average rate for each direction.

8. On a round trip of 396 km in each direction, the average rate of travel going was 33 km/h more than the rate returning. Find the rate for each direction if the entire trip took 18 hours.

9. After driving for 420 km, Susan decreased her average rate of travel by 14 km/h and traveled 588 km more. Find each rate if the total trip took 24 hours.

10. After driving for 312 km, Helen increased her rate of travel by 13 km/h and traveled 520 km more. The total time for the trip was 13 hours. Find the rate for each part of the trip.

Rate-of-Work Problems

Name _____

Date _____ Period _____

Show a complete solution for each problem.

1. It takes 7 hours for John to paint a house. Jerry can paint the same house in 5 hours. How long will it take them to paint the house if they work together?

   t = time takes to paint house together $\frac{t}{7} + \frac{t}{5} = 1$ $12t = 35$ It will take them 2 h 55 min to paint the house.

   $\frac{12t}{35} = 1$ $t = 2\,^{11}/_{12}$

2. Mary can do a job in 8 hours that Joan needs 10 hours to do. How long will it take them to do the job if they work together?

3. An inlet pipe can fill a tank in 3 hours. It takes 11 hours for the drain pipe to empty the tank. How long will it take to fill the tank if both the inlet pipe and the drain pipe are open?

4. An inlet pipe can fill a tank in 4 hours. It takes 19 hours for the drain pipe to empty the tank. How long will it take to fill the tank if both the inlet pipe and the drain pipe are open?

5. Jane takes 4 hours to do a job that Alice can do in 3 hours. If Jane works $\frac{1}{2}$ hour before Alice joins her, how long will it take the two of them to finish the job?

6. Harry takes 5 hours to do a job that Wayne can do in 2 hours. If Harry works for 20 minutes before Wayne joins him, how long will it take the two of them working together to finish the job?

7. Together, two pipes can fill a vat in 9 hours 36 minutes. If the larger pipe takes 16 hours to fill the vat, how long does it take the smaller pipe to fill the vat?

8. Jim and Albert work together at the bank and can put a certain set of data into the computer in 3 hours 44 minutes. It takes Jim 8 hours to do this work alone. How long does it take Albert to do this job alone?

9. Monica takes $7\frac{1}{2}$ hours to do a job that Jessica can do in 5 hours. Geraldine can do the same job in 6 hours. How long will it take the three of them working together to do the job?

10. Harley takes 6 hours to do a job that his father can do in 3 hours. The father's boss can do the job in 2 hours. How long does it take the three of them working together to do the job?

Rate-of-Work Problems

Name _____

Date _____ Period _____

Show a complete solution for each problem.

1. It takes 7 hours for Hank to paint a house. Wally can paint the same house in 6 hours. How long will it take them to paint the house if they work together?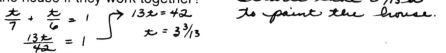

   t = time takes to paint house together

   $\frac{t}{7} + \frac{t}{6} = 1$

   $\frac{13t}{42} = 1$

   $13t = 42$

   $t = 3\frac{3}{13}$

   It will take $3\frac{3}{13}$ h to paint the house.

2. Linda can do a job in 5 hours that May does in 6 hours. How long will it take them to do the job if they work together?

3. An inlet pipe can fill a tank in 4 hours. It takes 6 hours for the drain pipe to empty the tank. How long will it take to fill the tank if both the inlet pipe and the drain pipe are open?

4. An inlet pipe can fill a tank in 9 hours. It takes 12 hours for the drain pipe to empty the tank. How long will it take to fill the tank if both the inlet pipe and the drain pipe are open?

5. Wilda can do a job in 4 hours that Karla needs 5 hours to do. If Wilda works 1 hour before Karla joins her, how long will it take the two of them to finish the job?

6. Juan takes 15 hours to do a job that his father can do in 6 hours. If Juan works for $4\frac{1}{2}$ hours before his father joins him, how long will it take the two of them working together to finish the job?

7. Together, two pipes can fill a vat in 8 hours 24 minutes. If the smaller pipe takes 28 hours to fill the vat, how long does it take the larger pipe to fill the vat?

8. Howard and Jim work together at the bank and can put a certain set of data into the computer in 2 hours 55 minutes. It takes Jim 5 hours to do this work alone. How long does it take Howard to do this job alone?

9. Juanita can do a job in 8 hours that Pauline takes 24 hours to do. Pauline's son can do the same job in 24 hours. How long will it take the three of them working together to do the job?

10. Hamilton takes 15 hours to do a job that his father can do in 8 hours. Mr. Wilson takes 24 hours to do the job. How long does it take the three of them working together to do the job?

Show a complete solution for each problem.

1. It takes 7 hours for Will to paint a house. Judy can paint the same house in 3 hours. How long will it take them to paint the house if they work together?   *It will take 2 h 6 min to paint the house.*

   t = time takes to paint house together

   $\frac{t}{7} + \frac{t}{3} = 1$ $10t = 21$, $t = 2\frac{1}{10}$

   $\frac{10t}{21} = 1$

2. Lupo can do a job in 4 hours that June does in 5 hours. How long will it take them to do the job if they work together?

3. An inlet pipe can fill a tank in 7 hours. It takes 10 hours for the drain pipe to empty the tank. How long will it take to fill the tank if both the inlet pipe and the drain pipe are open?

4. An inlet pipe can fill a tank in 5 hours. It takes 14 hours for the drain pipe to empty the tank. How long will it take to fill the tank if both the inlet pipe and the drain pipe are open?

5. Nancy can do a job in 8 hours that Wanda needs 13 hours to do. If Wanda works 3 hours 54 minutes before Nancy joins her, how long will it take the two of them to finish the job?

6. Sara takes 12 hours to do a job that her sister can do in 11 hours. If Sara works for 2 hours 48 minutes before her sister joins her, how long will it take the two of them working together to finish the job?

7. Together, two pipes can fill a vat in 2 hours 55 minutes. If the smaller pipe takes 7 hours to fill the vat, how long does it take the larger pipe to fill the vat?

8. Howard and Jim work together at the bank and can put a certain set of data into the computer in 3 hours 45 minutes. It takes Jim 6 hours to do this work alone. How long does it take Howard to do this job alone?

9. Dawn can do a job in 18 hours that Caroline takes 20 hours to do. Caroline's son can do the same job in 36 hours. How long will it take the three of them working together to do the job?

10. Connie takes 40 minutes to do a job that Kathleen can do in 35 minutes. Sheldon can do the job in 28 minutes. How long does it take the three of them working together to do the job?

Name _____

Date _____ Period _____

Show a complete solution for each problem.

1. It takes 15 hours for Wallace to paint a house. Paul can paint the same house in 5 hours. How long will it take them to paint the house if they work together? *It will take 3 h 45 min to paint the house.*

$t =$ *time takes to paint house together)* $\frac{t}{15} + \frac{t}{5} = 1$ $\frac{4t}{15} = 1$ $4t = 15$ $t = 3\frac{3}{4}$

2. Judith can do a job in 4 hours that Mike does in 6 hours. How long will it take them to do the job if they work together?

3. An inlet pipe can fill a tank in 6 hours. It takes 10 hours for the drain pipe to empty the tank. How long will it take to fill the tank if both the inlet pipe and the drain pipe are open?

4. An inlet pipe can fill a tank in 7 hours. It takes 15 hours for the drain pipe to empty the tank. How long will it take to fill the tank if both the inlet pipe and the drain pipe are open?

5. Matt can do a job in 4 hours that Wanda needs 6 hours to do. If Matt works $1\frac{1}{3}$ hours before Wanda joins him, how long will it take the two of them working together to finish the job?

6. Lysa takes 8 hours to do a job that her sister can do in 7 hours. If Lysa works 1 hour and 20 minutes before her sister joins her, how long will it take the two of them working together to finish the job?

7. Together, two pipes can fill a vat in 4 hours. If the larger pipe takes 6 hours to fill the vat, how long does it take the smaller pipe to fill the vat?

8. Stanley and Tom work together at the bank and can put a certain set of data into the computer in 4 hours 48 minutes. It takes Tom 8 hours to do this work alone. How long does it take Stanley to do this job alone?

9. Lucy can do a job in 4 hours that Caroline takes 3 hours to do. Hazel can also do the same job in 4 hours. How long will it take the three of them working together to do the job?

10. Shirley takes 30 minutes to do a job that Halley can do in 20 minutes. Charley can do the job in 36 minutes. How long does it take the three of them working together to do the job?

Equations in Two Variables

Name _____

Date _____ Period _____

Complete each table.

1. $4x + 2y = 10$

x	y
0	5
1	3
2	1
−1	7

2. $3x - y = 15$

x	y
0	
1	
2	
−1	

3. $y = 2x - 5$

x	y
0	
2	
−2	
−5	

4. $y = 8x + 7$

x	y
1	
5	
−3	
−5	

5. $4x - 3y = -18$

x	y
3	
6	
−3	
−6	

6. $7x - 8y = 32$

x	y
8	
24	
−16	
−32	

7. $x - 5y = 100$

x	y
10	
15	
−20	
−30	

8. $3x + 7y = 70$

x	y
7	
21	
−14	
−28	

9. $y = \frac{3}{4}x + 9$

x	y
8	
12	
−16	
0	

Developing Skills in Algebra   Book C

Equations in Two Variables

Name _____

Date _____ Period _____

Complete each table.

1. $y = \frac{7}{12}x + 19$

x	y
0	19
36	40
48	47
−60	−16

2. $11x - 2y = -22$

x	y
4	
10	
12	
−14	

3. $y = \frac{5}{3}x + 11$

x	y
6	
9	
−12	
−21	

4. $7x - 5y = -135$

x	y
5	
15	
25	
−30	

5. $3x - 4y = 124$

x	y
4	
12	
−8	
−20	

6. $y = \frac{9}{2}x + 12$

x	y
10	
20	
−26	
−32	

7. $4x - 15y = 450$

x	y
30	
60	
−60	
−75	

8. $3x + 13y = -169$

x	y
26	
52	
−39	
91	

9. $8x + 9y = -243$

x	y
27	
54	
−63	
−81	

Developing Skills in Algebra   Book C

Equations in Two Variables

Name _____

Date _____ Period _____

Complete each table.

1. $y = \dfrac{6}{7}x - 11$

x	y
7	-5
28	13
-35	-41
-42	-47

2. $8y - 5x = 80$

x	y
16	
32	
-8	
0	

3. $4x + 3y = -63$

x	y
9	
12	
-15	
-3	

4. $8x + 9y = 9$

x	y
18	
-9	
-18	
9	

5. $10y - 9x = 120$

x	y
10	
-10	
30	
-40	

6. $x - 5y = 15$

x	y
5	
25	
-10	
15	

7. $2x + 3y = 21$

x	y
3	
-3	
9	
0	

8. $5x - 6y = 18$

x	y
6	
-6	
18	
-12	

9. $7x - 16y = 48$

x	y
32	
-16	
-32	
0	

Developing Skills in Algebra   Book C

Equations in Two Variables

Name _____

Date _____ Period _____

Complete each table.

1. $5y - 17x = 25$

x	y
10	39
15	56
−5	−12
−60	−199

2. $11x + 16y = 32$

x	y
16	
−16	
32	
0	

3. $y = \dfrac{7}{8}x + 11$

x	y
8	
−8	
24	
0	

4. $y = \dfrac{5}{3}x - 14$

x	y
3	
−3	
9	
−12	

5. $3x + 4y = -36$

x	y
4	
8	
−12	
0	

6. $10x - 7y = 28$

x	y
7	
14	
−7	
0	

7. $2x - 3y = 63$

x	y
3	
−6	
−9	
0	

8. $y = \dfrac{11}{12}x + 4$

x	y
12	
−12	
24	
0	

9. $5x + 6y = -12$

x	y
6	
−12	
−18	
−24	

Developing Skills in Algebra   Book C

Graphing Linear Equations

Name _____

Date _____ Period _____

Graph two equations on each grid.

1. $3x - 4y = 7$

x	y
1	-1
-3	-4
5	2

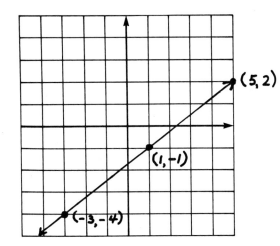

2. $3x - y = 2$

x	y

3. $x + 2y = 0$

x	y

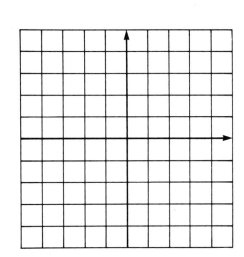

4. $2x - y = 2$

x	y

5. $2x + 3y = 6$

x	y

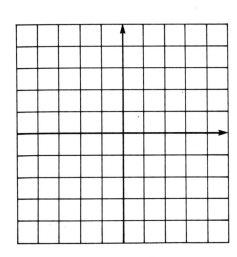

6. $3x + y = 1$

x	y

Developing Skills in Algebra   Book C

Name _____

Date _____ Period _____

Graph two equations on each grid.

1. $3x + 2y = -1$

x	y
1	-2
-1	1
-3	4

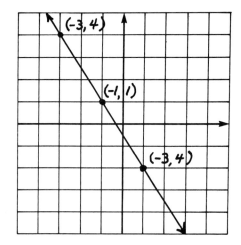

2. $2x - y = 4$

x	y

3. $2x - 3y = -6$

x	y

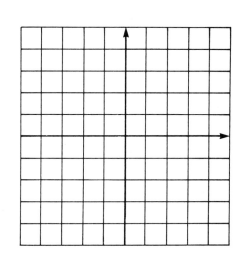

4. $4x + 3y = -8$

x	y

5. $x + y = 0$

x	y

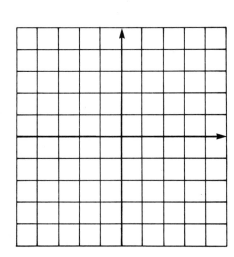

6. $2x - 5y = -10$

x	y

Graphing Linear Equations

Name _____

Date _____ Period _____

Graph two equations on each grid.

1. $2x - 3y = -5$

x	y
-4	-1
-1	1
2	3

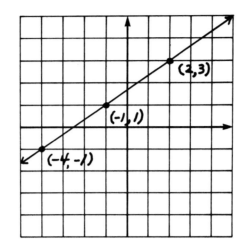

2. $y = -\frac{1}{4}x - 3$

x	y

3. $x + 2y = -2$

x	y

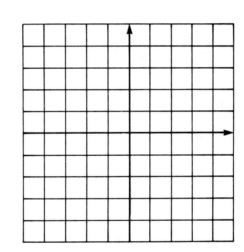

4. $3x - 4y = -12$

x	y

5. $2x - 3y = -3$

x	y

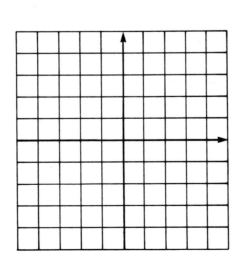

6. $x + 3y = 6$

x	y

Developing Skills in Algebra   Book C

Name _____

Date _____ Period _____

Graph two equations on each grid.

1. $x + 3y = -2$

x	y
1	-1
4	-2
-2	0

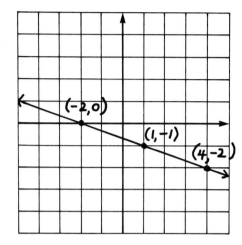

2. $2x + y = 1$

x	y

3. $y = -\dfrac{1}{2}x - \dfrac{7}{2}$

x	y

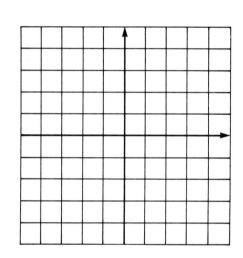

4. $3x - 4y = 4$

x	y

5. $5y - 4x = 5$

x	y

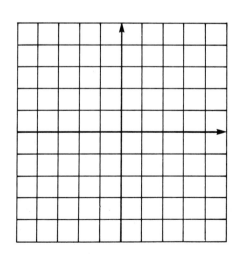

6. $x + 2y = -4$

x	y

Developing Skills in Algebra   Book C

Graphing in the Coordinate Plane

Name _____

Date _____ Period _____

State the slope of each line.

1.

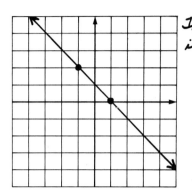

The slope is -1.

2.

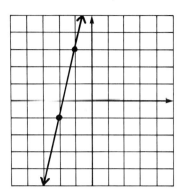

3.

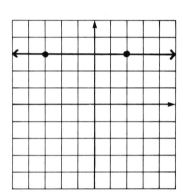

4.

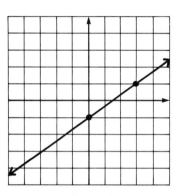

5.

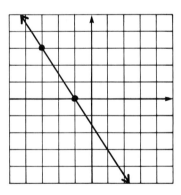

6.

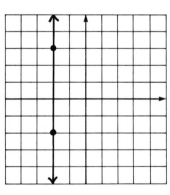

7.

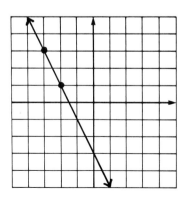

8.

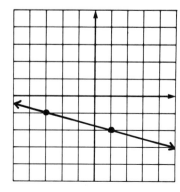

Graphing in the Coordinate Plane

Name _____

Date _____ Period _____

State the slope of each line.

1.

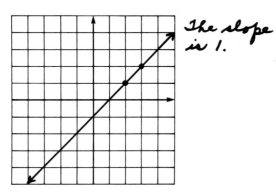

The slope is 1.

2.

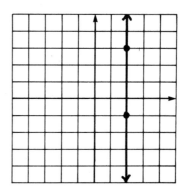

3.

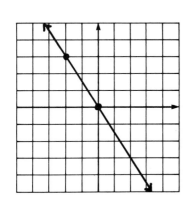

4.

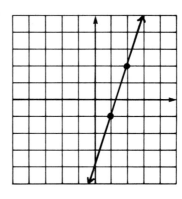

5.

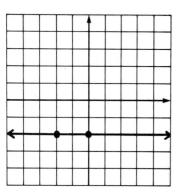

6.

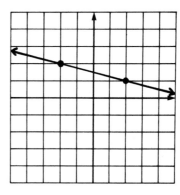

7.

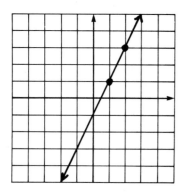

8.

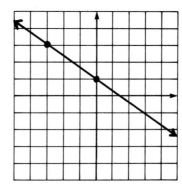

Developing Skills in Algebra   Book C

Slope of a Line

Name _____

Date _____ Period _____

State the slope of the line containing the given points.

1. (3, 4) and (−2, 3) *The slope is $\frac{1}{5}$.*

2. (−2, 5) and (−3, 6)

3. (1, 6) and (2, 3)

4. (4, −1) and (5, 3)

5. (−1, 4) and (3, 5)

6. (3, −3) and (3, −2)

7. (7, −2) and (8, −1)

8. (−6, 2) and (−4, −3)

9. (−4, −8) and (−4, 2)

10. (2, −5) and (7, 2)

11. (3, 5) and (−2, 5)

12. (−4, 3) and (−5, 8)

13. (−7, 6) and (3, 9)

14. (−1, 5) and (−3, 7)

15. (12, −15) and (10, −6)

16. (9, 2) and (−5, 2)

Graph the line with the given slope *m* containing the given point *P*.

17. $P = (0, 2); m = 1$

18. $P = (−2, 3); m = 2$

19. $P = (−3, −4); m = \frac{1}{2}$

20. $P = (0, −2); m = \frac{2}{3}$

21. $P = (2, −1); m = 0$

22. $P = (−4, 3); m = −3$

23. $P = (3, 2); m = 3$

24. $P = (−2, −2);$ no slope

25. $P = (4, −1); m = −\frac{3}{4}$

26. $P = (0, −3); m = −\frac{1}{2}$

27. $P = (3, 4);$ no slope

28. $P = (3, 4); m = 0$

29. $P = (0, 0); m = −2$

30. $P = (4, −1); m = \frac{1}{3}$

31. $P = (−3, 2); m = 4$

32. $P = (3, 3); m = −1$

Slope of a Line

State the slope of the line containing the given points.

1. (2, 1) and (3, 2) *The slope is 1.*

2. (−4, 2) and (−3, 1)

3. (2, 4) and (2, 5)

4. (6, −3) and (5, −4)

5. (−3, 6) and (3, −6)

6. (4, −2) and (5, −2)

7. (5, −1) and (8, −3)

8. (−4, 3) and (−4, −3)

9. (−2, −5) and (−4, −5)

10. (−2, −2) and (1, 2)

11. (2, 5) and (−3, 0)

12. (−1, 3) and (−5, 3)

13. (−2, 4) and (1, 3)

14. (−5, 5) and (−2, 1)

15. (10, −1) and (10, −7)

16. (7, −2) and (0, 2)

Graph the line with the given slope m containing the given point P.

17. $P = (0, -3); m = 1$

18. $P = (-1, 4); m = -2$

19. $P = (-2, -1); m = -\dfrac{1}{2}$

20. $P = (-3, -2); m = \dfrac{1}{3}$

21. $P = (-3, 1); m = 3$

22. $P = (0, 3); m = -1$

23. $P = (1, 2);$ no slope

24. $P = (-3, -4); m = 4$

25. $P = (3, -4); m = -\dfrac{2}{3}$

26. $P = (2, -3); m = 0$

27. $P = (0, -2); m = -3$

28. $P = (2, 0);$ no slope

29. $P = (1, 3); m = 0$

30. $P = (4, -1); m = \dfrac{1}{3}$

31. $P = (-1, -1); m = 3$

32. $P = (4, -3); m = -1$

Equations in Two Variables

Solve each equation for y and state the slope and y-intercept.

1. $3x + y = 5$ $y = -3x + 5$
$m = -3, b = 5$

2. $2x + y = 3$

3. $x + 3y = 9$

4. $x + 2y = 8$

5. $4x - y = 1$

6. $5x - y = 3$

7. $x - 4y = 16$

8. $x - 5y = 10$

9. $2x + 3y = 6$

10. $3x + 2y = 10$

11. $5x - 4y = 8$

12. $7x - 5y = 15$

13. $3x + 2y = 5$

14. $7x + 5y = 2$

15. $4x - 7y = 10$

16. $6x - 7y = 9$

17. $5x + 2y = 13$

18. $4x - 6y = 8$

19. $4x - 8y = 10$

20. $2x - 5y = 13$

Write an equation, in standard form, having the given slope and y-intercept.

21. $m = 4; b = 1$ $4x - y = -1$

22. $m = 2; b = -2$

23. $m = \frac{1}{2}; b = -3$

24. $m = \frac{2}{3}; b = -1$

25. $m = \frac{3}{2}; b = \frac{5}{2}$

26. $m = -\frac{3}{5}; b = 0$

27. $m = 1; b = -4$

28. $m = 0; b = 3$

29. $m = \frac{3}{5}; b = 0$

30. $m = -\frac{1}{2}; b = \frac{2}{3}$

31. $m = -2; b = -3$

32. $m = -\frac{3}{2}; b = \frac{5}{3}$

33. $m = 0; b = \frac{3}{4}$

34. $m = 3; b = \frac{2}{3}$

Equations in Two Variables

Name _____

Date _____ Period _____

Solve each equation for y and state the slope and y-intercept.

1. $4x + y = 2$ $y = -4x + 2$
$m = -4,\ b = 2$

2. $3x + y = 1$

3. $x + 2y = 10$

4. $x + 7y = 14$

5. $3x - y = 2$

6. $2x - y = 4$

7. $x - 2y = 10$

8. $x - 3y = 15$

9. $3x + 2y = 12$

10. $2x + 5y = 20$

11. $4x - 7y = 21$

12. $6x - 8y = 8$

13. $2x + 3y = 10$

14. $4x + 5y = 11$

15. $7x - 8y = 9$

16. $5x - 7y = 3$

17. $3x + 2y = 11$

18. $9x - 4y = 2$

19. $5x - 8y = 12$

20. $3x - 10y = 16$

Write an equation, in standard form, having the given slope and y-intercept.

21. $m = 2;\ b = 3$ $2x - y = -3$

22. $m = 3;\ b = -1$

23. $m = \dfrac{2}{3};\ b = -2$

24. $m = \dfrac{1}{2};\ b = 4$

25. $m = -1;\ b = 0$

26. $m = 0;\ b = -2$

27. $m = -\dfrac{1}{2};\ b = -4$

28. $m = -5;\ b = \dfrac{2}{3}$

29. $m = 4;\ b = \dfrac{1}{3}$

30. $m = \dfrac{3}{2};\ b = 0$

31. $m = -\dfrac{3}{4};\ b = \dfrac{5}{4}$

32. $m = \dfrac{1}{4};\ b = -\dfrac{2}{3}$

33. $m = -\dfrac{1}{3};\ b = \dfrac{5}{4}$

34. $m = -4;\ b = -1$

Developing Skills in Algebra   Book C

Equations in Two Variables   Name _____

                              Date _____ Period _____

Write an equation, in standard form, containing the given point and having the given slope.

1. $(3, 1); m = 2$ $2x - y = 5$ **2.** $(4, 2); m = -3$

3. $(2, 2); m = -1$ **4.** $(1, 3); m = 1$

5. $(-1, 3); m = 3$ **6.** $(0, -1); m = -2$

7. $(-2, 1); m = \dfrac{1}{2}$ **8.** $(-3, -2); m = \dfrac{2}{3}$

9. $(1, -4); m = 0$ **10.** $(1, -3); m = -\dfrac{5}{2}$

11. $(0, -3); m = -\dfrac{3}{4}$ **12.** $(3, -2); m = -\dfrac{1}{3}$

13. $(-3, -2); m = \dfrac{5}{2}$ **14.** $(-4, 1); m = \dfrac{5}{3}$

15. $(-1, -3); m = \dfrac{1}{3}$ **16.** $(3, 0); m = \dfrac{1}{4}$

17. $(1, 0); m = -\dfrac{4}{3}$ **18.** $(-2, -5); m = 0$

19. $(-2, 3); m = \dfrac{1}{5}$ **20.** $(-1, 4); m = \dfrac{1}{3}$

Write an equation, in standard form, containing the given points.

21. $(1, 1); (3, 2)$ $x - 2y = -1$ **22.** $(5, 3); (1, 4)$

23. $(3, 4); (3, -1)$ **24.** $(4, 1); (5, 3)$

25. $(-1, -2); (0, 0)$ **26.** $(0, 2); (4, 4)$

27. $(-2, -3); (0, -3)$ **28.** $(-3, 7); (-6, 3)$

29. $(3, -1); (2, -3)$ **30.** $(0, 0); (-2, 5)$

31. $(2, -1); (5, 0)$ **32.** $(-3, 0); (1, 2)$

33. $(0, -5); (4, 3)$ **34.** $(3, -2); (4, 0)$

       Developing Skills in Algebra   Book C

Equations in Two Variables

Name _____

Date _____ Period _____

Write an equation, in standard form, containing the given point and having the given slope.

1. $(2, 2); m = 1$ $x - y = 0$

2. $(2, 1); m = 1$

3. $(1, 3); m = 3$

4. $(1, 4); m = 4$

5. $(-2, 1); m = -1$

6. $(0, -2); m = 0$

7. $(-1, -3); m = 2$

8. $(-2, -1); m = -3$

9. $(1, 0); m = \dfrac{1}{3}$

10. $(0, 4); m = \dfrac{1}{2}$

11. $(3, -2); m = 0$

12. $(2, -2); m = -\dfrac{3}{4}$

13. $(0, -3); m = -\dfrac{2}{3}$

14. $(1, -3); m = \dfrac{1}{5}$

15. $(-2, -1); m = \dfrac{3}{2}$

16. $(0, -3); m = \dfrac{5}{3}$

17. $(1, 2); m = \dfrac{4}{3}$

18. $(4, -1); m = \dfrac{6}{5}$

19. $(-3, 0); m = -\dfrac{1}{2}$

20. $(2, -3); m = -\dfrac{3}{2}$

Write an equation, in standard form, containing the given points.

21. $(1, 3); (2, 4)$ $x - y = -2$

22. $(2, 3); (5, 2)$

23. $(2, 1); (1, 3)$

24. $(4, 2); (4, -1)$

25. $(3, -2); (5, 1)$

26. $(0, 4); (-2, 3)$

27. $(4, -1); (0, 0)$

28. $(4, -3); (3, -3)$

29. $(0, -2); (-1, -4)$

30. $(-2, 1); (-2, 5)$

31. $(5, 2); (5, -3)$

32. $(-2, -4); (3, 1)$

33. $(4, -3); (3, 0)$

34. $(-1, -2); (5, 2)$

Equations in Two Variables   Name _____

                                    Date _____ Period _____

Use the slope and *y*-intercept to graph each equation. Identify each graph by writing the equation on the line.

1. $x + y = 5$ **2.** $x + y = 3$

3. $x - y = 1$ **4.** $x - y = 4$

5. $2x + y = 2$ **6.** $3x + y = 3$

7. $2x - 3y = 6$ **8.** $3x - 2y = 6$

9. $4x + 3y = 9$ **10.** $2x + 3y = 12$

11. $x - 3y = 12$ **12.** $3x - 5y = 10$

13. $2x - 5y = 15$ **14.** $3x - 4y = 16$

15. $3x - 5y = -10$ **16.** $x - 3y = -9$

17. $2x - 6y = -12$ **18.** $5x - 3y = -15$

1–3.   **4–6.**   **7–9.**

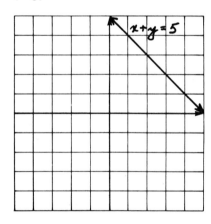   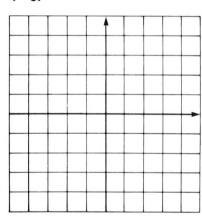   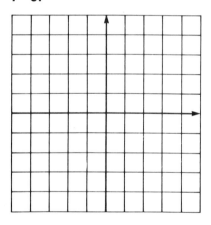

10–12.   **13–15.**   **16–18.**

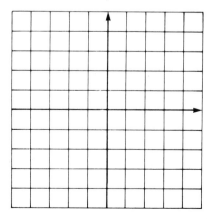   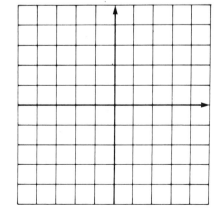   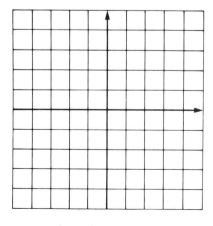

                   Developing Skills in Algebra   Book C

Equations in Two Variables

Use the slope and *y*-intercept to graph each equation. Identify each graph by writing the equation on the line.

1. $x + y = 2$ **2.** $x + y = 4$

3. $x - y = 3$ **4.** $x - y = 5$

5. $3x + y = 4$ **6.** $2x + y = 3$

7. $3x - 2y = 2$ **8.** $2x - 3y = 6$

9. $5x + 2y = 10$ **10.** $3x - 4y = 12$

11. $x - 4y = 8$ **12.** $2x - 5y = 10$

13. $3x + 2y = 10$ **14.** $4x + 2y = -8$

15. $2x + 3y = -6$ **16.** $x - 4y = -8$

17. $5x - 2y = 4$ **18.** $4x + 3y = 6$

1–3.

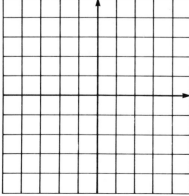

4–6.

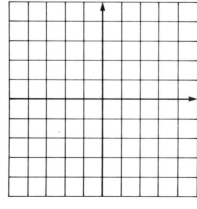

7–9.

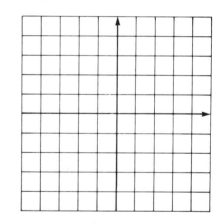

10–12.

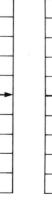

13–15.

16–18.

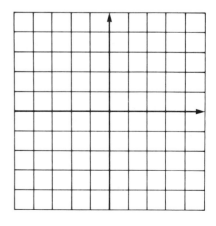

Developing Skills in Algebra   Book C

Solving Equations with Two Variables   Name _____

                                            Date _____ Period _____

Solve each pair of equations by graphing.

1. $x - y = -1$ $(1, 2)$
$2x + y = 4$

2. $2x - 3y = -3$
$2x + 3y = 3$

3. $x + 2y = 4$
$3x - 2y = 4$

4. $x - 4y = 4$
$3x + y = -1$

5. $3x + 3y = 3$
$x + 3y = -3$

6. $x - y = -3$
$2x + y = 0$

7. $3x + y = -2$
$3x - 2y = 4$

8. $x + 4y = 3$
$4x - y = -5$

9. $x - 2y = -2$
$2x - y = 2$

10. $3x - 2y = -3$
$3x - 2y = 1$

11. $2x - 3y = 4$
$x - 3y = 5$

12. $3x - 4y = -3$
$2x - y = 3$

13. $2x - 3y = -7$
$y = 3$

14. $y = 2x + 1$
$4x - 2y = -2$

15. $y = 3x$
$3x - y = 3$

16. $x = -2$
$4x + 3y = -2$

17. $y = x + 3$
$3x + y = -1$

18. $2x + y = 3$
$x - 4y = 6$

19. $y = -3x - 2$
$3x + y = 3$

20. $y = 2x + 2$
$4x + y = 8$

21. $2x + 3y = 8$
$6y = 16 - 4x$

22. $2x + y = 5$
$2y = x$

23. $3x - 2y = -4$
$3x = 2y - 4$

24. $3y = x$
$4x - 3y = -9$

59   Developing Skills in Algebra   Book C

Solving Equalities with Two Variables   Name _____

                                               Date _____ Period _____

Solve each pair of equations by graphing.

1. $2x + 3y = 6$ **(0, 2)**
   $2x - y = -2$

2. $3x + y = -3$
   $x - y = -1$

3. $x - 3y = -3$
   $5x - 3y = 9$

4. $x + y = 1$
   $x - 2y = 4$

5. $x - 2y = -4$
   $3x = 2y$

6. $2x + y = -4$
   $5x - 2y = -1$

7. $3x - 2y = -6$
   $3x = 2y + 2$

8. $y = -2x$
   $y = x + 3$

9. $2x - y = -2$
   $3y = 6x + 6$

10. $y = 2$
   $4x - 5y = -2$

11. $3y = 9 - 5x$
   $5x + 3y = -9$

12. $2x + y = -5$
   $y = 2x + 3$

13. $y = x + 2$
   $3x - y = 2$

14. $3x + y = 4$
   $y = -3x - 2$

15. $3x - y = -7$
   $3x - 5y = 1$

16. $2x - 7y = -24$
   $2x - 3y = -8$

17. $4x - 3y = -5$
   $8x = 6y - 10$

18. $x - 2y = -4$
   $2y = 3x$

19. $3x - 2y = 3$
   $x = 3$

20. $3x - 2y = -3$
   $3x = 2y + 4$

21. $x + 2y = 3$
   $2x - y = -4$

22. $y = 3x + 3$
   $x - y = 1$

23. $x - 3y = -11$
   $5x + 2y = -4$

24. $x - y = -2$
   $y = 2x + 1$

---

60   Developing Skills in Algebra   Book C

Solving Equations with Two Variables   Name _____

                                              Date _____ Period _____

Solve each pair of equations by substitution.

1. $x - y = 3$
$x + y = 5$ **(4, 1)**

2. $2x + y = 1$
$-x - 2y = -5$

3. $x - 5 = y$
$2x - 3y = 7$

4. $x - 4y = -1$
$3x + 5y = 31$

5. $x - y = 3$
$2x - 3y = -3$

6. $2x + 3y = -13$
$4x + y = -1$

7. $x + 2y = 11$
$12x - 6y = 12$

8. $3x - 5y = -4$
$4x + 2y = 12$

9. $6x + y = 14$
$10x - y = 2$

10. $2x + 5y = 7$
$x - y = -7$

11. $2x - 4y = 0$
$3x - y = 15$

12. $2x + y = 3$
$4x + 3y = 1$

13. $2x - 3y = 6$
$y - 6x = 14$

14. $6x + 5y = 11$
$x + y = 1$

15. $4x + 3y = 2$
$y + 2x = 6$

16. $6x + y = 0$
$2x + y = -2$

17. $2x - 4y = -2$
$x + 4y = -4$

18. $9x + 2y = 9$
$y - 6x = 1$

19. $3x - 4y = 10$
$2y + 4x = 6$

20. $4x + 3y = -1$
$2x + y = 1$

21. $2x - 4y = 1$
$4x - 6y = 2$

22. $2x + 4y = 6$
$x + 4y = 2$

23. $4x + 5y = 2$
$4x - 20y = -3$

24. $x - 3y = 0$
$4x + 8y = 5$

Solving Equations with Two Variables

Solve each pair of equations by substitution.

1. $x - y = 7$
$x + y = 9$ $(8, 1)$

2. $3x - y = 5$
$x + 3y = 5$

3. $x - y = -2$
$4x - 3y = 4$

4. $2x - 3y = 3$
$x + 4y = 7$

5. $x - y = 6$
$2x - 3y = 20$

6. $2x - y = 8$
$3x - y = 6$

7. $x + 3y = 7$
$4x - 5y = -6$

8. $4x - 3y = 5$
$3x + 6y = 12$

9. $4x + y = -19$
$7x - y = 8$

10. $5x + 6y = 10$
$2x - y = 4$

11. $3x - y = 5$
$4x - y = 3$

12. $3x + 4y = -20$
$x - 5y = 6$

13. $6x - 5y = 4$
$y - 4x = 2$

14. $7x + 3y = 20$
$x + y = 4$

15. $5x + 2y = -30$
$3x - y = 4$

16. $3x + 6y = 16$
$x + 3y = 5$

17. $3x - 7y = 22$
$5x - y = 2$

18. $2x + 3y = 73$
$x - 5y = 4$

19. $2x - y = 5$
$3x + 7y = -1$

20. $3x - 4y = 7$
$x - 3y = 2$

21. $4x - 12y = 1$
$4x - 7y = 6$

22. $5x + 3y = 15$
$2x - 3y = -1$

23. $2x - 5y = 2$
$6x + 5y = 2$

24. $3x - 2y = 0$
$5x + 4y = 11$

Developing Skills in Algebra   Book C

Solving Equations with Two Variables   Name _____

                                            Date _____ Period _____

Solve each pair of equations by addition or subtraction.

1. $x + y = 10$
$x - y = 8$ $(9, 1)$

2. $x + y = 13$
$x - y = 7$

3. $x + 3y = 7$
$3x + 3y = 9$

4. $x + 5y = -11$
$2x + 5y = -12$

5. $3x + y = 5$
$6x + 2y = 10$

6. $4x + 3y = 0$
$5x - 3y = 27$

7. $5x + 2y = -8$
$3x - 2y = -8$

8. $3x - 2y = -4$
$6x + 5y = 37$

9. $4x - 5y = -9$
$2x + 3y = 1$

10. $2x - 3y = 4$
$4x - 6y = 8$

11. $x + 3y = 7$
$x + 3y = -4$

12. $5x - 3y = -18$
$x - 6y = -9$

13. $3x - 2y = 12$
$2x + y = 1$

14. $4x - y = -14$
$3x + 2y = -16$

15. $4x - 7y = -30$
$5x - 7y = -34$

16. $3x - y = -2$
$3x - y = -1$

17. $3x + 2y = 9$
$3x + 4y = 3$

18. $4x + 3y = 19$
$7x - 6y = -23$

19. $5x - 3y = -36$
$2x + 3y = 15$

20. $4x + 5y = 2$
$2x - 5y = 16$

21. $3x + y = 13$
$6x + 2y = 26$

22. $2x - 3y = 20$
$11x + 2y = -1$

23. $4x - 7y = -5$
$3x - 2y = -7$

24. $3x + 2y = -1$
$4x - 5y = -32$

Solving Equations with Two Variables

Name _____

Date _____ Period _____

Solve each pair of equations by addition or subtraction.

1. $2x + 3y = 11$
$3x - 4y = -9$ $(1, 3)$

2. $6x - 5y = 43$
$3x + 2y = -1$

3. $3x - y = 9$
$x + 2y = -4$

4. $3x + 7y = -33$
$5x - 2y = -14$

5. $5x - 2y = -1$
$3x + 4y = -11$

6. $2x - 7y = 24$
$5x + 2y = -18$

7. $2x - 3y = -11$
$4x + 7y = 43$

8. $7x + 3y = -6$
$4x - 5y = -37$

9. $x + 4y = 1$
$2x - 5y = 15$

10. $3x + 2y = 10$
$3x + 2y = 7$

11. $4x - 5y = -1$
$4x - 5y = 0$

12. $4x - 7y = -37$
$3x + 5y = 3$

13. $3x - 2y = 3$
$4x + 3y = -13$

14. $3x - 4y = -29$
$2x + 5y = 19$

15. $6x + 5y = -8$
$2x - 7y = 32$

16. $2x - 5y = 9$
$4x - 10y = 18$

17. $5x - 4y = 32$
$3x + 2y = 6$

18. $7x - 4y = 13$
$14x - 8y = 10$

19. $7x + 9y = 50$
$3x - 7y = -22$

20. $2x - 6y = -22$
$x + 4y = 17$

21. $6x - 5y = 9$
$12x - 10y = 11$

22. $3x - 5y = -14$
$2x + 7y = 1$

23. $4x - 3y = -41$
$5x + 2y = -11$

24. $3x - 2y = 4$
$4x + 5y = -10$

Developing Skills in Algebra   Book C

Solving Equations with Two Variables   Name _____

                                              Date _____ Period _____

Solve each pair of equations by addition or subtraction.

1. $5x - 2y = 12$ **(2, −1)**
$5x - 4y = 14$

2. $x + 4y = -18$
$2x - 3y = 8$

3. $7x - 4y = 15$
$14x - 8y = 30$

4. $3x - 4y = 27$
$3x + 4y = 3$

5. $2x + 3y = -3$
$2x - 7y = -13$

6. $3x + 2y = -16$
$7x + 9y = -33$

7. $6x - 5y = -2$
$2x + 7y = -18$

8. $7x + 3y = 4$
$21x - 9y = 12$

9. $3x - 7y = -35$
$3x + 5y = 25$

10. $3x - y = -1$
$2x - 3y = -10$

11. $x + 2y = 11$
$4x - 3y = 0$

12. $3x + 7y = -9$
$3x - 4y = -9$

13. $4x - 12y = 2$
$2x - 6y = 1$

14. $2x - 5y = 3$
$4x - 10y = 6$

15. $4x + 3y = 7$
$4x + 3y = -7$

16. $4x + 7y = 1$
$2x - 7y = -4$

17. $15x + 6y = 13$
$12x - 10y = 3$

18. $3x - 2y = -1$
$3x - 2y = 5$

19. $2x - 5y = -23$
$6x + 5y = -9$

20. $3x + 2y = 20$
$3x - 5y = -29$

21. $15x + 10y = -4$
$5x - 2y = 4$

22. $5x + 2y = -3$
$10x + 4y = 2$

23. $2x - 3y = 10$
$2x - 3y = -4$

24. $3x - 2y = 0$
$24x - 30y = -7$

---

65   Developing Skills in Algebra   Book C

Solving Equations with Two Variables

Name _____

Date _____ Period _____

Solve each pair of equations by addition or subtraction.

1. $2x - 3y = 7$
   $2x + 4y = 0$ $(2, -1)$

2. $2x + 3y = 0$
   $3x + y = -7$

3. $x + y = 0$
   $3x - y = 12$

4. $5x + 2y = 4$
   $5x + 2y = -10$

5. $4x + 3y = 7$
   $8x + 6y = 14$

6. $3x + 4y = 19$
   $6x + 5y = 26$

7. $x + 3y = -5$
   $2x + y = -10$

8. $6x - 4y = -6$
   $3x - 2y = -3$

9. $5x - 3y = 10$
   $5x - 3y = 13$

10. $5x - 3y = 13$
   $x - 6y = 8$

11. $3x + y = -11$
   $3x - 2y = -14$

12. $4x - 5y = 1$
   $11x + 2y = -13$

13. $3x + 2y = 19$
   $4x - 5y = 10$

14. $x + 5y = -2$
   $x + 5y = -7$

15. $3x - 2y = 2$
   $6x - 4y = 4$

16. $12x - 3y = -6$
   $4x - y = -2$

17. $4x - 7y = 5$
   $4x - 7y = -13$

18. $7x - 6y = 12$
   $4x + 3y = -6$

19. $2x - 3y = 0$
   $10x - 6y = 3$

20. $2x + 5y = 6$
   $2x - 5y = 2$

21. $10x - 14y = 47$
   $3x + 2y = 11$

22. $4x + 5y = 3$
   $5x + 2y = 8$

23. $3x - 2y = 12$
   $2x - y = 9$

24. $6x - 30y = 13$
   $2x + 3y = 0$

Developing Skills in Algebra   Book C

Name _____

Date _____ Period _____

Use two equations with two variables to solve each problem.

1. The sum of two numbers is 18 and their difference is 12. Find each of the numbers.

$x = $ greater number $\quad x + y = 18$ $\Big\}$ $2x = 30$ $\quad (15) + y = 18$ $\quad$ The numbers
$y = $ lesser number $\quad x - y = 12$ $\qquad x = 15$ $\qquad y = 3$ $\quad$ are 15 and 3.

2. The sum of two numbers is 26 and their difference is 20. Find each of the numbers.

3. The sum of two numbers is 34 and their difference is 14. Find each of the numbers.

4. The sum of two numbers is 28 and their difference is 6. Find each of the numbers.

5. The sum of two numbers is 42 and their difference is 30. Find each of the numbers.

6. The sum of two numbers is 80 and their difference is 22. Find each of the numbers.

7. The sum of two numbers is 15 less than twice the first number. Their difference is 5 less than twice the second number. Find each of the numbers.

8. The sum of two numbers is 8 less than twice the first number. Their difference is 4 less than twice the second number. Find each of the numbers.

9. The sum of two numbers is 10 less than three times the first number. Their difference is 5 less than twice the second number. Find each of the numbers.

10. The sum of two numbers is 6 less than twice the first number. Their difference is 10 less than four times the second number. Find each of the numbers.

Name _____

Date _____ Period _____

Use two equations with two variables to solve each problem.

1. The sum of two numbers is 36 and their difference is 8. Find each of the numbers.

x = greater number $\left.\begin{array}{l} x + y = 36 \\ x - y = 8 \end{array}\right\}$ → $\begin{array}{l} 2x = 44 \\ x = 22 \end{array}$ $\begin{array}{l} (22) + y = 36 \\ y = 14 \end{array}$ The two numbers

y = lesser number   are 22 and 14.

2. The sum of two numbers is 27 and their difference is 3. Find each of the numbers.

3. The sum of two numbers is 57 and their difference is 5. Find each of the numbers.

4. The sum of two numbers is 108 and their difference is 16. Find each of the numbers.

5. The sum of two numbers is 38 and their difference is 16. Find each of the numbers.

6. The sum of two numbers is 125 and their difference is 47. Find each of the numbers.

7. The sum of two numbers is 18 less than twice the first number. Their difference is 32 less than twice the second number. Find each of the numbers.

8. The sum of two numbers is 23 less than twice the first number. Their difference is 19 less than twice the second number. Find each of the numbers.

9. The sum of two numbers is 3 more than four times the first number. Their difference is 10 less than twice the second number. Find each of the numbers.

10. The sum of two numbers is 13 more than twice the first number. Their difference is 14 less than the second number. Find each of the numbers.

Perimeter Problems

Name _____

Date _____ Period _____

Use two equations with two variables to solve each problem.

1. The perimeter of a rectangle is 32 cm. The length is 1 cm more than twice the width. Find the dimensions of the rectangle.

   $2l + 2w = 32$ $\quad 2l + (l-1) = 32$ $\quad 2w + 1 = (11)$

   $l = length$ $\qquad l = 2w + 1$ $\qquad\quad 3l - 1 = 32$ $\qquad 2w = 10$

   $w = width$ $\qquad\qquad\qquad\qquad\qquad 3l = 33$ $\qquad\qquad w = 5$

   $\qquad\qquad\qquad\qquad\qquad\qquad\qquad l = 11$ $\qquad$ The rectangle is

   $\qquad\qquad\qquad\qquad\qquad\qquad\qquad\qquad\qquad\qquad$ 5 cm × 11 cm.

2. The perimeter of a rectangle is 56 cm. The length of the rectangle is 2 cm more than the width. Find the dimensions of the rectangle.

3. The perimeter of a rectangle is 42 m. The length of the rectangle is 3 m more than twice the width. Find the dimensions of the rectangle.

4. The perimeter of a rectangle is 62 cm. The length of the rectangle is 1 cm more than twice the width. Find the dimensions of the rectangle.

5. The perimeter of a rectangle is 76 cm. The length of the rectangle is 2 cm more than twice the width. Find the dimensions of the rectangle.

6. The perimeter of a rectangle is 66 m. The length is 1 m more than three times the width. Find the dimensions of the rectangle.

7. The perimeter of a rectangle is 84 m. The length is $2\frac{1}{2}$ times the width. Find the dimensions of the rectangle.

8. The perimeter of a rectangle is 52 m. The length is $2\frac{1}{4}$ times the width. Find the dimensions of the rectangle.

9. The perimeter of a rectangle is 58 cm. The length of the rectangle is 1 cm more than $2\frac{1}{2}$ times the width. Find the dimensions of the rectangle.

10. The perimeter of a rectangle is 64 cm. The length of the rectangle is 2 cm more than $1\frac{1}{2}$ times the width. Find the dimensions of the rectangle.

Developing Skills in Algebra   Book C

Perimeter Problems

Name _____

Date _____ Period _____

Use two equations with two variables to solve each problem.

1. The perimeter of a rectangle is 44 cm. The length is 2 cm more than three times the width. Find the dimensions of the rectangle.

$l = length$ $2l + 2w = 44$ } $2(3w+2) + 2w = 44$ $l = 3(5) + 2$

$w = width$ $l = 3w + 2$ } $8w + 4 = 44$ $= 17$ The rectangle is

$8w = 40$ $5 cm \times 19 cm.$

$w = 5$

2. The perimeter of a rectangle is 74 cm. The length of the rectangle is 5 cm less than twice the width. Find the dimensions of the rectangle.

3. The perimeter of a rectangle is 122 m. The length of the rectangle is 11 m less five times the width. Find the dimensions of the rectangle.

4. The perimeter of a rectangle is 98 m. The length of the rectangle is 9 m more than four times the width. Find the dimensions of the rectangle.

5. The perimeter of a rectangle is 108 cm. The width of the rectangle is 6 cm less than the length. Find the dimensions of the rectangle.

6. The perimeter of a rectangle is 24 m. The width is 30 m less than five times the length. Find the dimensions of the rectangle.

7. The perimeter of a rectangle is 37 m. The length is 1 m less than twelve times the width. Find the dimensions of the rectangle.

8. The perimeter of a rectangle is 22 cm. The length is $1\frac{3}{4}$ times the width. Find the dimensions of the rectangle.

9. The perimeter of a rectangle is 30 m. The length of the rectangle is 3 m more than twice the width. Find the dimensions of the rectangle.

10. The perimeter of a rectangle is 20 cm. The length of the rectangle is 3 cm less than $2\frac{1}{4}$ times the width. Find the dimensions of the rectangle.

Age Problems

Use two equations with two variables to solve each problem.

1. Mrs. Bruce lacks 1 year from being 5 times as old as her son. Five years from now she will lack 1 year from being 3 times as old as her son will be then. Find each of their ages.

   b = mrs. Bruce's age $b = 5s - 1$ $(5s-1)+5 = 3(s+5)-1$ $b = 5(5)-1$

   s = son's age $b+5 = 3(s+5)-1$ $2s = 10$ $= 24$

                                         $s = 5$ mrs. Bruce is 24 and her son is 5.

2. Mr. Lopez is 1 year more than 3 times as old as his daughter. Six years from now, he will lack 1 year from being $2\frac{1}{2}$ times as old as she will be then. Find each of their ages.

3. Mrs. Johnson is 3 times as old as her son. Ten years ago she was 5 times as old as her son was then. Find each of their ages.

4. Mr. King is 4 times as old as his daughter. Four years ago he was 6 times as old as his daughter was then. Find each of their ages.

5. The sum of 4 times Joan's age and 3 times Jim's age is 47. Jim is 1 year less than twice as old as Joan. Find each of their ages.

6. The sum of 6 times Jack's age and 5 times Larry's age is 63. Jack is 1 year less than 3 times as old as Larry. Find each of their ages.

7. The sum of 4 times Lisa's age and 7 times Jane's age is 169. Jane is 1 year more than twice as old as Lisa is. Find each of their ages.

8. The sum of 6 times Petra's age and 8 times Kathy's age is 162. Kathy is 1 year more than twice as old as Petra is. Find each of their ages.

9. The sum of 3 times Darlene's age and 7 times Sharon's age is 173. Darlene is 2 years less than twice as old as Sharon is. Find each of their ages.

10. The sum of 6 times Jennifer's age and 5 times James' age is 150. James is 2 years less than twice as old as Jennifer is. Find each of their ages.

            Developing Skills in Algebra   Book C

Age Problems

Name _____

Date _____ Period _____

Use two equations with two variables to solve each problem.

1. Mr. Entz lacks 1 year from being 4 times as old as his son. Fifteen years from now he will be 4 years more than 2 times as old as his son will be then. Find both of their ages.

   e = Mr. Entz' age $e = 4s - 1$ } $(4s-1) + 15 = 4 + 2(s + 15)$
   s = son's age $e + 15 = 4 + 2(s + 15)$ }

2. Mrs. Garcia is 1 year less than 3 times as old as her daughter. Seven years from now, she will be 4 years more than twice as old as her daughter will be then. Find both of their ages.

3. Mr. Jackson is 13 years less than 3 times as old as his son. Six years ago, he was 14 years more than twice as old as his son was then. Find each of their ages.

4. Mrs. Kwok is 6 years more than 3 times as old as her daughter. Eight years ago she was 2 years less than 9 times as old as her daughter was then. Find each of their ages.

5. The sum of 3 times John's age and 2 times Jill's age is 44. Jill is 8 years less than twice as old as John is. Find each of their ages.

6. The sum of 4 times Mike's age and 3 times Susan's age is 79. Mike is 1 year more than 3 times as old as Susan. Find each of their ages.

7. The sum of 3 times Don's age and 5 times Sean's age is 150. Sean is 9 years less than twice as old as Don is. Find each of their ages.

8. The sum of 7 times Paul's age and 4 times Kent's age is 111. Kent is 1 year less than four times as old as Paul is. Find each of their ages.

9. The sum of 5 times Doug's age and 2 times Sheldon's age is 152. Doug is 6 years older than Sheldon is. Find each of their ages.

10. The sum of 4 times Kelly's age and 5 times Kent's age is 128. Kent is 4 years older than Kelly is. Find each of their ages.

Digit Problems

Use two equations with two variables to solve each problem.

1. A certain two-digit number has a value that is 1 more than 5 times the sum of its digits. The units digit is 1 more than the tens digit. Find the number.

$u = $ units digit $\qquad u + 10t = 5(u+t) + 1$

$t = $ tens digit $\qquad u = t + 1$

$(t+1) + 10t = 5[(t+1) + t] + 1$

$11t + 1 = 10t + 6$

$t = 5$

$u = (5) + 1 = 6$

The number is 56.

2. A certain two-digit number has a value that is 2 more than 6 times the sum of its digits. The tens digit is 1 more than the units digit. Find the number.

3. The value of a certain two-digit number is 5 times the sum of its digits. If the digits are reversed, the resulting number is 9 more than the original number. Find the original number.

4. The value of a certain two-digit number is 9 times the sum of its digits. If the digits are reversed, the resulting number is 63 less than the original number. Find the original number.

5. The sum of the digits of a certain two-digit number is 10. If the number formed by interchanging the digits is subtracted from the original number, the result is 18. Find the original number.

6. The sum of the digits of a certain two-digit number is 6. If the original number is subtracted from the number formed by interchanging the digits, the result is 36. Find the original number.

7. The tens digit of a certain two-digit number is 1 more than 3 times the units digit. The original number is 9 less than 3 times the number formed by interchanging the digits. Find the original number.

8. The units digit of a certain two-digit number is one more than 4 times the tens digit. The number formed by interchanging the digits is 6 more than 3 times the original number. Find the original number.

9. A certain two-digit number is 2 more than 4 times the units digit. If the digits of the number are interchanged, the resulting number is 10 more than twice the original number. Find the original number.

10. A certain two-digit number is 13 more than 9 times the tens digit. The original number is 4 less than twice the number formed by interchanging the digits. Find the original number.

Developing Skills in Algebra   Book C

Use two equations with two variables to solve each problem.

1. A certain two-digit number has a value that is 3 more than 4 times the sum of its digits. The units digit is two more than the tens digit. Find the number.

   $(2+t) + 10t = 4[(2+t) + t] + 3$

   $u = \text{units digit}$ $u + 10t = 4(u+t) + 3$

   $t = \text{tens digit}$ $u = 2 + t$

   $11t + 2 = 8t + 11$

   $3t = 9$

   $t = 3$

   $u = 2 + (3)$

   $= 5$

   The number is 35.

2. A certain two-digit number has a value that is 8 less than 5 times the sum of its digits. The tens digit is 3 less than the units digit. Find the number.

3. The value of a certain two-digit number is 2 times the sum of its digits. If the digits are reversed, the resulting number is $4\frac{1}{2}$ times the original number. Find the original number.

4. The value of a certain two-digit number is 4 more than 6 times the sum of its digits. If the digits are reversed, the resulting number is 18 less than the original number. Find the original number.

5. The sum of the digits of a certain two-digit number is 5. If the number formed by interchanging the digits is subtracted from the original number, the result is -9. Find the original number.

6. The sum of the digits of a certain two-digit number is 8. If the original number is subtracted from the number formed by interchanging the digits, the result is -18. Find the original number.

7. The tens digit of a certain two-digit number is two more than the units digit. The original number is 18 more than the number formed by interchanging the digits. Find the original number.

8. The units digit of a certain two-digit number is one more than 2 times the tens digit. The number formed by interchanging the digits is 4 less than 2 times the original number. Find the original number.

9. A certain two-digit number is 2 more than 3 times the units digit. If the digits of the number are interchanged, the resulting number is 24 less than 4 times the original number. Find the original number.

10. A certain two-digit number is 4 more than 10 times the tens digit. The original number is 10 less than twice the number formed by interchanging the digits. Find the original number.

Money Problems

Name _____

Date _____ Period _____

Use two equations with two variables to solve each problem.

1. The cost of 3 boxes of envelopes and 4 boxes of note paper is $13.25. Two boxes of envelopes and 6 boxes of note paper cost $17. Find the cost of each box of envelopes and each box of note paper.

$e = cost\ of\ envelopes$
$w = cost\ of\ note\ paper$

$\left. \begin{array}{l} 3e + 4w = 13.25 \\ 2e + 6w = 17.00 \end{array} \right\}$ $\begin{array}{l} 6e + 8w = 28.50 \\ 6e + 18w = 51.00 \\ \hline -10w = -22.50 \\ w = 2.25 \end{array}$ $\begin{array}{l} 2e + 6(2.25) = 17.00 \\ 2e = 3.50 \\ e = 1.75 \end{array}$

The envelopes cost $1.75.
The note paper cost $2.25.

2. The cost of 8 boxes of small paper clips and 7 boxes of large paper clips is $44.95. Five boxes of small clips and 3 boxes of large ones cost $22.80. Find the cost of a box of each size of paper clips.

3. The cost of 12 oranges and 7 apples is $5.36. Eight oranges and 5 apples cost $3.68. Find the cost of each orange and each apple.

4. The cost of 8 avocados and 3 tomatoes is $8.39. Four avocados and 12 tomatoes cost $11.44. Find the cost of each avocado and each tomato.

5. The cost of 5 tables and 20 chairs is $739.70. The cost of 7 tables and 42 chairs is $1378.44. Find the cost of each table and each chair.

6. The cost of 5 bedspreads and 8 pillows is $431.67. Three bedspreads and 10 pillows cost $344.75. Find the cost of each bedspread and each pillow.

7. Three pairs of jeans and six shirts cost $104.25. The cost of 4 pairs of jeans and 5 shirts is $112.15. Find the cost of each pair of jeans and each shirt.

8. The cost of 2 pairs of athletic shoes and 5 pairs of shorts is $105.88. The cost of 3 pairs of athletic shoes and 2 pairs of shorts is $98.43. Find the cost of each pair of shoes and each pair of shorts.

9. The cost of 5 sixty-minute cassette tapes and 9 ninety-minute tapes is $71.40. The cost of 8 sixty-minute tapes and 7 ninety-minute tapes is $74.65. Find the cost of each type of tape.

10. The cost of 8 adult's tickets and 7 children's tickets is $82.45. The cost of 6 adult's tickets and 9 children's tickets is $78.15. Find the cost of each adult's ticket and each child's ticket.

Money Problems

Use two equations with two variables to solve each problem.

1. The cost of 5 boxes of envelopes and 6 boxes of note paper is $16.75. Three boxes of envelopes and 4 boxes of note paper cost $10.75. Find the cost of each box of envelopes and each box of note paper.

$$5e + 6w = 16.75$$
$$3e + 4w = 10.75$$

$$10e + 12w = 33.50$$
$$9e + 12w = 32.50$$
$$e \qquad = 1.25$$

$$5(1.25) + 6w = 16.75$$
$$6w = 10.50$$
$$w = 1.75$$

$e = cost\ of\ envelopes$
$w = cost\ of\ note\ paper$

The envelopes cost $1.25.
The note paper cost $1.75.

2. The cost of 4 boxes of small paper clips and 9 boxes of large paper clips is $15.75. Eight boxes of small clips and 7 boxes of large ones cost $16.65. Find the cost of a box of each size of paper clips.

3. The cost of 24 oranges and 15 apples is $12.36. Fifteen oranges and 12 apples cost $8.67. Find the cost of each orange and each apple.

4. The cost of 5 avocados and 6 tomatoes is $7.15. Three avocados and 8 tomatoes cost $6.27. Find the cost of each avocado and each tomato.

5. The cost of 4 tables and 15 chairs is $904.80. The cost of 2 tables and 10 chairs is $549.90. Find the cost of each table and each chair.

6. The cost of 3 bedspreads and 6 pillows is $539.73. Two bedspreads and 4 pillows cost $359.82. Find the cost of each bedspread and each pillow.

7. Two pairs of jeans and three shirts cost $133.00. The cost of 3 pairs of jeans and 6 shirts is $231.00. Find the cost of each pair of jeans and each shirt.

8. The cost of 4 pairs of athletic shoes and 6 pairs of shorts is $144.60. The cost of 2 pairs of athletic shoes and 4 pairs of shorts is $79.80. Find the cost of each pair of shoes and each pair of shorts.

9. The cost of 8 sixty-minute cassette tapes and 5 ninety-minute tapes is $35.67. The cost of 10 sixty-minute tapes and 2 ninety-minute tapes is $31.20. Find the cost of each type of tape.

10. The cost of 6 adult's tickets and 12 children's tickets is $210.00. The cost of 4 adult's tickets and 8 children's tickets is $140.00. Find the cost of each adult's ticket and each child's ticket.

Motion Problems

Name _____

Date _____ Period _____

Use two equations with two variables to solve each problem.

1. In Grape Creek, Jim can row 30 km downstream in 3 hours or he can row 18 km upstream in the same amount of time. Find the rate he rows in still water and the rate of the current.

s = rate in still water $3(s+c) = 30$ $3s + 3c = 30$ $3(8) + 3c = 30$
c = rate of current $3(s-c) = 18$ $3s - 3c = 18$ $3c = 6$
$6s = 48$ $c = 2$
$s = 8$ Jim rows 8 km/hr in
still water and the
current moves at 2 km/hr.

2. In Prairie Dog Creek, Geri can row 60 km downstream in 4 hours or she can row 36 km upstream in the same amount of time. Find the rate she rows in still water and the rate of the current.

3. In Blue River, Terry can row 36 km downstream in 3 hours but it takes him 6 hours to row that same distance upstream. Find the rate he rows in still water and the rate of the current.

4. In Thompson Creek, Emmy can row 48 km downstream in 4 hours but it takes her 6 hours to row that same distance upstream. Find the rate she rows in still water and the rate of the current.

5. Joe flew his small airplane 900 km in 5 hours flying with the wind. He flew 700 km against the wind in 7 hours. Find the rate at which he flew in still air and the rate of the wind.

6. Patricia flew a small plane for 3 hours with the wind and traveled 585 km. The return trip against the wind took 5 hours. Find the rate at which she flew in still air and the rate of the wind.

7. A jet liner flying east with the wind traveled 3600 km in 6 hours. The return trip, flying against the wind, took 8 hours. Find the rate at which the jet flew in still air and the rate of the wind.

8. A jet liner flying east with the wind traveled 4200 km in 7 hours. The return trip, flying against the wind, took 10 hours. Find the rate at which the jet flew in still air and the rate of the wind.

Motion Problems

Name _____

Date _____ Period _____

Use two equations with two variables to solve each problem.

1. In Grape Creek, Ham can row 27 km downstream in 3 hours or he can row 15 km upstream in the same amount of time. Find the rate he rows in still water and the rate of the current.

w = rate in still water
c = rate of current

$3(w+c) = 27$
$3(w-c) = 15$

$3w + 3c = 27$
$3w - 3c = 15$
$6w = 42$
$w = 7$

$3(8) + 3c = 27$
$3c = 3$
$c = 1$

Ham rows 7 km/hr in still water and the current moves at 1 km/hr.

2. In Prairie Dog Creek, June can row 50 km downstream in 5 hours or she can row 25 km upstream in the same amount of time. Find the rate she rows in still water and the rate of the current.

3. In Blue River, Jackie can row 32 km downstream in 8 hours but it takes him 4 hours to row 12 km upstream. Find the rate he rows in still water and the rate of the current.

4. In Thompson Creek, Edna can row 28 km downstream in 4 hours but it takes her 7 hours to row that same distance upstream. Find the rate she rows in still water and the rate of the current.

5. Ben flew his small airplane 660 km in 6 hours flying with the wind. He flew 350 km against the wind in 7 hours. Find the rate at which he flew in still air and the rate of the wind.

6. Angela flew a small plane for 5 hours with the wind and traveled 700 km. The return trip against the wind took 7 hours. Find the rate at which she flew in still air and the rate of the wind.

7. A jet liner flying east with the wind traveled 3000 km in 5 hours. The return trip, flying against the wind, took 6 hours 15 minutes. Find the rate at which the jet flew in still air and the rate of the wind.

8. A jet liner flying east with the wind traveled 2800 km in 4 hours 40 minutes. The return trip, flying against the wind, took 7 hours. Find the rate at which the jet flew in still air and the rate of the wind.

Name _____

Date _____ Period _____

Use two equations in two variables to solve each problem.

1. If the temperature on a Celsius scale is multiplied by four and added to three times the reading on a Fahrenheit scale, the result is 284. Five times the Celsius reading plus two times the Fahrenheit reading is 236. Find the temperature on each scale.

c = Celsius temp.
f = Fahrenheit temp.

$$\begin{array}{r} 4c + 3f = 284 \\ 5c + 2f = 236 \end{array} \Big\}$$

$$\begin{array}{r} 8c + 6f = 568 \\ 15c + 6f = 708 \\ \hline -7c = -140 \\ c = 20 \end{array}$$

$$4(20) + 3f = 284$$
$$3f = 204$$
$$f = 68$$

The temperature is 68°F and 20°C.

2. If the temperature on a Celsius scale is multiplied by four and added to three times the reading on a Fahrenheit scale, the result is 566. Eight times the Celsius reading plus four times the Fahrenheit reading is 888. Find the temperature on each scale.

3. If the temperature on a Celsius scale is multiplied by six and added to five times the reading on a Fahrenheit scale, the result is 10. Five times the Celsius reading plus three times the Fahrenheit reading is −8. Find the temperature on each scale.

4. If the temperature on a Celsius scale is multiplied by five and added to two times the reading on a Fahrenheit scale, the result is 21. Three times the Celsius reading plus the Fahrenheit reading is 8. Find the temperature on each scale.

5. If the temperature on a Celsius scale is multiplied by eight and added to three times the reading on a Fahrenheit scale, the result is 431. Five times the Celsius reading minus two times the Fahrenheit reading equals −29. Find the temperature on each scale.

6. If the temperature on a Celsius scale is multiplied by seven and added to three times the reading on a Fahrenheit scale, the result is 158. Three times the Celsius reading minus four times the Fahrenheit reading equals −149. Find the temperature on each scale.

7. If the temperature on a Celsius scale is multiplied by three and added to two times the reading on a Fahrenheit scale, the result is 526. If the Fahrenheit reading is subtracted from twice the Celsius reading, the result is −18. Find the temperature on each scale.

8. If the temperature on a Celsius scale is multiplied by four and added to three times the reading on a Fahrenheit scale, the result is 237. If the Fahrenheit reading is subtracted from three times the Celsius reading, the result is −14. Find the temperature on each scale.

Temperature Problems

Name _____

Date _____ Period _____

Use two equations in two variables to solve each problem.

1. If the temperature on a Celsius scale is multiplied by three and added to four times the reading on a Fahrenheit scale, the result is 434. Six times the Celsius reading plus two times the Fahrenheit reading is 352. Find the temperature on each scale.

$$c = \text{Celsius temp.}$$
$$f = \text{Fahrenheit temp.}$$

$$\left. \begin{array}{l} 3c + 4f = 434 \\ 6c + 2f = 352 \end{array} \right\} \quad \begin{array}{l} 6c + 8f = 868 \\ \underline{6c + 2f = 352} \\ \quad 6f = 516 \\ \quad f = 86 \end{array}$$

$$3c + 4(86) = 434$$
$$3c = 90$$
$$c = 30$$

The temperature is $86°F$ and $30°C$.

2. If the temperature on a Celsius scale is multiplied by two and added to twice the reading on a Fahrenheit scale, the result is 568. Eight times the Celsius reading plus three times the Fahrenheit reading is 1302. Find the temperature on each scale.

3. If the temperature on a Celsius scale is multiplied by eight and added to four times the reading on a Fahrenheit scale, the result is 508. Three times the Celsius reading plus three times the Fahrenheit reading is 306. Find the temperature on each scale.

4. If the temperature on a Celsius scale is multiplied by two and added to four times the reading on a Fahrenheit scale, the result is 82. Nine times the Celsius reading plus the Fahrenheit reading is −22. Find the temperature on each scale.

5. If the temperature on a Celsius scale is multiplied by eight and added to three times the reading on the Fahrenheit scale, the result is 699. Five times the Celsius reading minus two times the Fahrenheit reading equals −1. Find the temperature on each scale.

6. If the temperature on a Celsius scale is multiplied by two and added to the reading on a Fahrenheit scale, the result is 412. Five times the Celsius reading minus four times the Fahrenheit reading equals −348. Find the temperature on each scale.

7. If the temperature on a Celsius scale is multiplied by six and added to two times the reading on a Fahrenheit scale, the result is 688. If the Fahrenheit reading is subtracted from twice the Celsius reading, the result is −19. Find the temperature on each scale.

8. If the temperature on a Celsius scale is multiplied by five and added to two times the reading on a Fahrenheit scale, the result is 795. If two times the Fahrenheit reading is subtracted from six times the Celsius reading, the result is 140. Find the temperature on each scale.

Developing Skills in Algebra   Book C

Name _____

Date _____ Period _____

Use two equations in two variables to solve each problem.

1. Candy worth $1.05 a pound was mixed with candy worth $1.35 a pound to produce a mixture worth $1.17 a pound. How many pounds of each kind of candy were used to make 30 pounds of the mixture?

   $x =$ am't 1.05 candy
   $y =$ am't 1.35 candy

   $1.05x + 1.35y = 1.17(x+y)$
   $x + y = 30$

   $1.05(30-y) + 1.35y = 1.17(30)$
   $31.5 + 0.3y = 35.1$
   $0.3y = 3.6$
   $y = 12$
   $x + (12) = 30$
   $x = 18$

   There are 18 lb of 1.05 candy and 12 lb of 1.35 candy.

2. Peanuts worth $2.25 a pound were mixed with cashews worth $3.25 a pound to produce a mixture worth $2.65 a pound. How many pounds of each kind of nuts were used to produce 35 pounds of the mixture?

3. Coffee worth $3.75 a pound was mixed with coffee worth $4.35 a pound to produce a blend worth $4.11 a pound. How much of each kind of coffee was used to produce 40 pounds of blended coffee?

4. Dried apricots worth $3.25 a pound were mixed with dried prunes worth $4.79 a pound to produce a mixture of dried fruit worth $3.79 a pound. How much of each kind of fruit was used to produce 25 pounds of mixture?

5. A 12% brine solution was mixed with a 16% brine solution to produce a 15% brine solution. How much of the 12% solution and how much of the 16% solution were used to produce 40 L of the 15% solution?

6. A 3% solution of sulfuric acid was mixed with an 18% solution of sulfuric acid to produce an 8% solution. How much 3% solution and how much 18% solution were used to produce 15 L of 8% solution?

7. Pure copper was mixed with a 10% copper alloy to produce an alloy that was 25% copper. How much of the pure copper and how much 10% alloy were used to produce 36 kg of 25% alloy?

8. Pure tin was mixed with a 4% tin alloy to produce an alloy that was 16% tin. How much pure tin and how much 4% alloy were used to produce 32 kg of 16% alloy?

81

Mixture Problems

Name _____

Date _____ Period _____

Use two equations in two variables to solve each problem.

1. Candy worth $1.25 a pound was mixed with candy worth $1.50 a pound to produce a mixture worth $1.35 a pound. How many pounds of each kind of candy were used to make 45 pounds of the mixture?

$1.25x + 1.50y = 1.35(x+y)$ $1.25(45-y) + 1.50y = 1.35(45)$ There are 27 lb
$x + y = 45$ $56.25 + 0.25y = 60.75$ of $1.25 candy
$x = $am't $1.25 candy $0.25y = 4.50$ and 18 lb of
$y = $am't $1.50 candy $y = 18$ $1.50 candy.
$x + (18) = 45$
$x = 27$

2. Peanuts worth $2.90 a pound were mixed with cashews worth $4.60 a pound to produce a mixture worth $3.50 a pound. How many pounds of each kind of nuts were used to produce 51 pounds of the mixture?

3. Coffee worth $2.95 a pound was mixed with coffee worth $3.50 a pound to produce a blend worth $3.30 a pound. How much of each kind of coffee was used to produce 44 pounds of blended coffee?

4. Dried apricots worth $5.75 a pound were mixed with dried prunes worth $3.80 a pound to produce a mixture of dried fruit worth $4.25 a pound. How much of each kind of fruit was used to produce 52 pounds of mixture?

5. A 25% brine solution was mixed with an 18% brine solution to produce a 20% brine solution. How much of the 25% solution and how much of the 18% solution were used to produce 28 L of the 20% solution?

6. A 2% solution of sulfuric acid was mixed with a 12% solution of sulfuric acid to produce an 8% solution. How much 2% solution and how much 12% solution were used to produce 10 L of 8% solution?

7. Pure copper was mixed with a 12% copper alloy to produce an alloy that was 32% copper. How much of the pure copper and how much 12% alloy were used to produce 44 kg of 32% alloy?

8. Pure tin was mixed with an 8% tin alloy to produce an alloy that was 25% tin. How much pure tin and how much 8% alloy were used to produce 184 kg of 25% alloy?

Name _____

Date _____ Period _____

Use two equations in two variables to solve each problem.

1. The sum of two numbers is 51 and their difference is 13. Find each of the numbers.

x = greater number   *x + y = 51*   *(32) + y = 51*   *The two numbers are*
y = lesser number   *x − y = 13*   *y = 19*   *32 and 19.*
                      2x   = 64
                        x = 32

2. The perimeter of a rectangle is 68 cm. The length is four cm more than the width. Find the dimensions of the rectangle.

3. Mrs. Brook lacks 7 years from being five times as old as her son. Six years from now she will lack 3 years from being three times as old as her son is then. Find each of their ages.

4. One number is five more than three times a smaller one. If four times the larger number is subtracted from twice the smaller one, the result is 0. Find each of the numbers.

5. One number is four more than another number. The difference between five times the smaller number and six times the larger number is 5. Find each of the numbers.

6. A certain two-digit number has a value that is three times the sum of its digits. The units digit is one more than three times the tens digit. Find the number.

7. The cost of 5 boxes of envelopes and 5 boxes of note paper is $25.95. Two boxes of envelopes and 6 boxes of note paper cost $22.38. Find the cost of each box of envelopes and each box of note paper.

8. In Colorado Creek, Darrell can row 24 km downstream in 6 hours or he can row 18 km upstream in the same amount of time. Find the rate he rows in still water and the rate of the current.

9. If the temperature on a Celsius scale is divided by five it is equal to the reading on a Fahrenheit scale. Fifteen times the Fahrenheit reading is equal to three times the Celsius reading. Find the temperature on each scale.

10. Candy worth $0.95/kg was mixed with candy worth $1.85/kg to produce a mixture worth $1.45/kg. How many kilograms of each kind of candy were used to make 27 kg of the mixture?

Miscellaneous Word Problems

Name _____

Date _____ Period _____

Use two equations in two variables to solve each problem.

1. The sum of two numbers is 76 and their difference is 54. Find each of the numbers.

x = greater number $x + y = 76$ $(65) + y = 76$ The two numbers
y = lesser number $x - y = 54$ $y = 11$ are 65 and 11.
                              $2x = 130$
                                 $x = 65$

2. The perimeter of a rectangle is 114 centimeters. The length is 6 centimeters less than twice the width. Find the dimensions of the rectangle.

3. Mr. Diaz is 1 year more than three times as old as his daughter. Four years from now he will lack 7 years from being three times as old as his daughter is then. Find each of their ages.

4. The smaller of two numbers is eight less than three times the larger number. If twice the smaller number is added to 15, the result is 11. Find each of the numbers.

5. The larger of two numbers is seven more than twice the smaller number. If five times the larger number is subtracted from 12, the result is 17. Find each of the numbers.

6. A certain two-digit number has a value that is seven more than six times the sum of its digits. The tens digit is 3 more than the units digit. Find the number.

7. The cost of 5 boxes of small paper clips and 2 boxes of large paper clips is $49.30. Seven boxes of small clips and 4 boxes of large ones cost $79.10. Find the cost of a box of each size of paper clips.

8. In Red River, Karen can row 12 km downstream in 45 minutes or she can row $1\frac{1}{2}$ km upstream in the same amount of time. Find the rate she rows in still water and the rate of the current.

9. If the temperature on a Celsius scale is multiplied by three and added to two times the reading on a Fahrenheit scale, the result is 460. Five times the Celsius reading plus four times the Fahrenheit reading is equal to 860. Find the temperature on each scale.

10. Peanuts worth $2.95/kg were mixed with cashews worth $6.25/kg to produce a mixture worth $5.00/kg. How many kilograms of each kind of nuts were used to make 33 kg of the mixture?

Miscellaneous Word Problems

Name _____

Date _____ Period _____

Use two equations in two variables to solve each problem.

1. The sum of two numbers is 94 and their difference is 122. Find each of the numbers.

x = greater number $x + y = 94$ $(108) + y = 94$ The two numbers

y = lesser number $x - y = 122$ $y = -14$ are 108 and -14.

$2x = 216$

$x = 108$

2. The perimeter of a rectangle is 132 meters. The length is 2 m more than three times the width. Find the dimensions of the rectangle.

3. Mrs. Johnson is five times as old as her son. Three years ago she was eight times as old as her son was then. Find each of their ages.

4. The smaller of two numbers is nine less than five times the larger number. If four times the smaller number is subtracted from 7, the result is 43. Find each of the numbers.

5. One number is five more than three times a second number. If 10 is added to -2 times the first number, the result is 30. Find each of the numbers.

6. The value of a certain two-digit number is four less than six times the sum of its digits. If the digits of the number are reversed, the resulting number is nine less than the original number. Find the number.

7. The cost of 10 oranges and 5 apples is $3.35. Twenty-four oranges and 12 apples cost $8.04. Find the cost of each orange and each apple.

8. Bill flew his small airplane 459 km in $4\frac{1}{2}$ hours flying with the wind. He flew 480 km against the wind in 6 hours. Find the rate at which he flew in still air and the rate of the wind.

9. If the temperature on a Fahrenheit scale is multiplied by three and subtracted from eight times the reading on a Celsius scale, the result is 34. Two times the Celsius reading plus the Fahrenheit reading is 222. Find the temperature on each scale.

10. A 9% solution of sulfuric acid was mixed with a 30% solution of sulfuric acid to produce an 18% solution. How much 9% solution and how much 30% solution were used to make 21 L of 18% solution?

Miscellaneous Word Problems

Name _____

Date _____ Period _____

Use two equations in two variables to solve each problem.

1. The sum of two numbers is 40 and their difference is 190. Find each of the numbers.

x = greater number $x + y = 40$ $(115) + y = 40$ The two numbers
y = lesser number $\underline{x - y = 190}$ $y = -75$ are 115 and -75.
                          $2x = 230$
                          $x = 115$

2. The perimeter of a rectangle is 90 cm. The length is 15 cm more than four times the width. Find the dimensions of the rectangle.

3. Mr. King is two times as old as his daughter. Ten years ago he lacked 5 years from being three times as old as his daughter was then. Find each of their ages.

4. The larger of two numbers is three less than four times the smaller number. If eight times the larger number is subtracted from 20, the result is −20. Find each of the numbers.

5. The smaller of two numbers is three more than −2 times the larger one. If four times the smaller number is subtracted from the larger number, the result is 51. Find the numbers.

6. The value of a certain two-digit number is eight times the sum of its digits. If the digits of the number are reversed, the result is 45 less than the original number. Find the original number.

7. The cost of 4 avocados and 5 tomatoes is $3.76. Six avocados and 3 tomatoes cost $4.02. Find the cost of each avocado and each tomato.

8. Linda flew a small plane for 3 hours with the wind and traveled 492 km. The return trip against the wind took 6 hours. Find the rate at which she flew in still air and the rate of the wind.

9. If the temperature on a Celsius scale is multiplied by four and added to two times the reading on a Fahrenheit scale, the result is 178. Eight times the Celsius reading plus five times the Fahrenheit reading is 415. Find the temperature on each scale.

10. Pure copper was mixed with a 12% alloy to produce an alloy that was 20% copper. How much of the pure copper and how much 12% alloy were used to produce 132 kg of the 20% alloy?

Solving Inequalities

Name _____

Date _____ Period_____

Solve

1. $3x < 9$ $x < 3$

2. $5x > 25$

3. $x + 3 > 8$

4. $x + 4 < 12$

5. $x - 7 < 10$

6. $x - 4 > 18$

7. $3x + 5 < 23$

8. $6x + 8 \geq 44$

9. $7x - 2 > 47$

10. $9x - 3 < 51$

11. $-x < 7$

12. $-x > 6$

13. $4 - x > 11$

14. $15 - x < 15$

15. $9 - x \geq 13$

16. $8 - 4x > 48$

17. $2x < 6$

18. $3x > 15$

19. $x + 1 > 4$

20. $x + 3 < 10$

21. $x - 9 < 12$

22. $x - 7 > 15$

23. $2x + 7 < 15$

24. $4x + 5 > 15$

25. $3x - 1 > 14$

26. $7x - 4 < 24$

27. $-x < 5$

28. $-x > 2$

29. $5 - x \geq 7$

30. $12 - x < 13$

31. $8 - x > 15$

32. $9 - 5x > 39$

Solving Inequalities

Name _____

Date _____ Period _____

Solve.

1. $4x < 8$ $x < 2$ 2. $2x < 8$

3. $x + 7 > 10$ 4. $x + 20 > -1$

5. $x - 9 < 12$ 6. $x - 9 < -13$

7. $4x + 7 < 39$ 8. $3x + 9 < 39$

9. $9x - 2 \geq 61$ 10. $5x - 4 > 46$

11. $-x < 9$ 12. $-x < -4$

13. $5 - x > 13$ 14. $6 - x \leq 19$

15. $7 - x > 16$ 16. $31 - 12x > 79$

17. $7x > 28$ 18. $13x > 39$

19. $x + 11 < 20$ 20. $x + 17 < -10$

21. $x - 19 > 26$ 22. $x - 21 \geq 19$

23. $7x + 5 > 82$ 24. $10x + 9 > 29$

25. $11x - 6 \leq 93$ 26. $15x - 5 < 70$

27. $-x < 14$ 28. $-x > 14$

29. $17 - x < 23$ 30. $14 - x < 23$

31. $14 - 6x > 74$ 32. $12 - 4x \geq 48$

Solving Inequalities   Name _____

                              Date _____ Period _____

_____

Solve.

1. $2(3x + 1) > -16$ $x > -3$ **2.** $4(2x - 3) < 52$

3. $7(3x - 9) < 126$ **4.** $2(4x - 4) > -72$

5. $3(5x - 5) > 60$ **6.** $7 - 3(7x - 5) < 1$

7. $14 - 5(7x + 3) \leq -71$ **8.** $7 - 4(2x - 8) > -9$

9. $19 - 4(x + 8) > 39$ **10.** $16 - 6(x + 12) < -2$

11. $13 + 4(5x - 7) < 25$ **12.** $10 + 2(5x - 3) \geq 94$

13. $-3 - 5(4x + 6) > 7$ **14.** $-15 - 8(5x + 3) < 41$

15. $3 + 4(2 - 6x) < 83$ **16.** $11 + 3(9 - 8x) > 158$

17. $-17 - 4(6 - 2x) \geq 23$ **18.** $-12 - 3(7 - 4x) \leq 3$

19. $16 + 2(5 + 7x) < -16$ **20.** $31 + 2(7 + 5x) > -15$

21. $32 - 5(1 - 4x) > -13$ **22.** $21 - 5(7 - 9x) < 121$

23. $15 + 7(2 - 4x) \leq -35$ **24.** $36 - 2(6 - 2x) > -16$

25. $45 + 4(11 - 6x) < -55$ **26.** $13 - 2(7 + 8x) > 79$

27. $22 - 5(9 + 6x) < 67$ **28.** $19 - 3(9 + 8x) \geq -80$

29. $11 - 7(11 + 8x) > 102$ **30.** $30 + 5(13 + 12x) < -25$

31. $22 + 2(20 - 6x) \leq -22$ **32.** $37 + 7(10 - 3x) > -40$

                                       Developing Skills in Algebra   Book C

Solving Inequalities

Name _____

Date _____ Period _____

Solve.

1. $3(5x + 2) > -24$ $x > -2$

2. $2(4x - 1) < 30$

3. $7(2x - 4) < 28$

4. $5(3x - 1) > -50$

5. $2(3x - 5) \geq 20$

6. $4 - 3(2x - 7) < -5$

7. $12 - 3(2x + 1) < -15$

8. $8 - 5(3x - 2) > 78$

9. $21 - 6(x + 7) > 9$

10. $15 - 4(x + 10) < 15$

11. $11 + 2(2x - 7) < 25$

12. $16 + 3(3x - 4) \geq 76$

13. $-7 - 8(5x + 3) > 9$

14. $-11 - 9(4x + 2) < 43$

15. $5 + 7(3 - 5x) < 77$

16. $12 + 8(7 - 6x) > 106$

17. $-13 - 2(4 - 3x) \geq 15$

18. $-17 - 5(9 - 6x) < 28$

19. $18 + 6(7 + 4x) < -12$

20. $21 + 3(9 + 7x) > -14$

21. $22 - 8(2 - 3x) > -54$

22. $41 - 6(5 - 5x) \leq 41$

23. $16 + 5(3 - 2x) \leq -9$

24. $26 - 4(4 - 3x) > -20$

25. $50 + 6(14 - 6x) < 14$

26. $15 - 5(2 + 7x) > -100$

27. $31 - 3(4 + 3x) < 26$

28. $21 - 6(3 + 5x) > -87$

29. $42 - 6(8 + 5x) > 114$

30. $81 - 5(2 + 8x) < -9$

31. $62 - 11(3 - 4x) \leq -15$

32. $56 - 4(12 - 6x) > -40$

Solving Absolute Value Equations

Name _____

Date _____ Period _____

Solve.

1. $|x| = 5$ $x = \pm 5$

2. $|x| = 7$

3. $|x| = 10$

4. $|x| = 25$

5. $|x| = 12$

6. $|x| = 9$

7. $|x| = 0$

8. $|x| = -4$

9. $|x| + 2 = 3$

10. $|x| + 5 = 13$

11. $|x| + 7 = 20$

12. $|x| + 13 = 30$

13. $|x| + 5 = 7$

14. $|x| + 3 = 10$

15. $|x| - 9 = 15$

16. $|x| - 11 = 20$

17. $|x| - 4 = 17$

18. $|x| - 10 = 15$

19. $|x| - 11 = 14$

20. $|x| - 14 = 21$

21. $|x| + 9 = 5$

22. $|x| + 12 = 24$

23. $|x + 2| = 7$

24. $|x + 5| = 12$

25. $|x| + 7 = 4$

26. $|x| + 19 = 29$

27. $|x + 4| = 13$

28. $|x + 7| = 25$

29. $|x - 9| = 2$

30. $|x - 13| = 10$

31. $|x + 3| = 11$

32. $|x + 14| = 20$

Solving Absolute Value Equations

Name _____

Date _____ Period _____

Solve.

1. $|x| = 8$ $x = \pm 8$ 2. $|x| = 12$

3. $|x| = 14$ 4. $|x| = 22$

5. $|x| = 13$ 6. $|x| = 29$

7. $|x| = -1$ 8. $|x| = 24$

9. $|x| + 3 = 7$ 10. $|x| + 2 = 11$

11. $|x| + 6 = 18$ 12. $|x| + 3 = 17$

13. $|x| + 9 = 21$ 14. $|x| + 10 = 20$

15. $|x| - 8 = 12$ 16. $|x| - 14 = 30$

17. $|x| - 14 = 26$ 18. $|x| - 22 = -9$

19. $|x| - 9 = 19$ 20. $|x| - 15 = 19$

21. $|x| + 3 = 7$ 22. $|x| + 14 = 28$

23. $|x| + 11 = 43$ 24. $|x| + 4 = 21$

25. $|x + 3| = 10$ 26. $|x + 4| = -25$

27. $|x + 4| = 13$ 28. $|x + 7| = 25$

29. $|x + 5| = 14$ 30. $|x + 6| = 24$

31. $|x - 7| = 3$ 32. $|x - 12| = 12$

Solving Absolute Value Equations

Name _____

Date _____ Period _____

Solve.

1. $|x - 11| = 22$ $x = 33 \text{ or } -11$

2. $|x - 13| = -5$

3. $|x + 7| - 5 = 13$

4. $|x + 9| - 3 = 17$

5. $|x - 4| = 13$

6. $|x + 7| + 5 = 15$

7. $|x - 3| + 2 = 18$

8. $|x - 5| + 7 = 10$

9. $-7|x + 2| = 49$

10. $|x + 9| - 16 = 20$

11. $|x - 2| + 4 = 10$

12. $|x - 3| - 11 = 24$

13. $2|x + 3| = 10$

14. $-4|x - 8| = 16$

15. $4|x - 7| = 32$

16. $3|x - 10| = 33$

17. $3|x - 4| = 24$

18. $4|x + 8| = 40$

19. $|x + 7| - 14 = 14$

20. $-10|x + 7| = 90$

21. $-5|x - 10| = 35$

22. $5|x + 7| = 30$

23. $|3x + 4| = 11$

24. $|7x + 3| = 18$

25. $|2x + 3| = 5$

26. $|3x + 1| = 7$

27. $|2x - 4| = -6$

28. $|5x - 2| = 8$

29. $|3x - 5| = 7$

30. $-6|x - 7| = 36$

31. $-4|x + 14| = 28$

32. $|6x - 7| = 29$

93

Solving Absolute Value Equations

Name _____

Date _____ Period _____

Solve.

1. $|x - 10| = 20$ $x = 30$ or -10

2. $|x - 17| = -9$

3. $|x + 5| - 4 = 11$

4. $|x + 3| - 8 = 19$

5. $|x - 4| = 30$

6. $|x + 12| = 39$

7. $|x - 2| + 6 = 13$

8. $|x - 2| + 6 = 18$

9. $|x + 5| - 12 = 17$

10. $|x + 5| - 10 = 25$

11. $|x + 7| = 35$

12. $|x - 3| + 7 = 12$

13. $-7|x - 14| = 35$

14. $6|x + 3| = 36$

15. $5|x - 8| = 45$

16. $-12|x + 3| = 84$

17. $4|x - 6| = 24$

18. $4|x + 2| = 28$

19. $-9|x + 1| = 45$

20. $2|x - 12| = 32$

21. $2|x + 4| = 16$

22. $-8|x - 9| = 16$

23. $-6|x + 12| = 18$

24. $|5x - 5| = 17$

25. $|2x + 2| = 6$

26. $|3x + 4| = 7$

27. $|2x - 6| = -6$

28. $-11|x - 8| = 33$

29. $|5x - 3| = 12$

30. $|4x + 6| = 14$

31. $|5x + 4| = 16$

32. $|4x - 8| = 20$

Name _____

Date _____ Period _____

Graph each set of real numbers.

1. $\{x: |x| > 2\}$

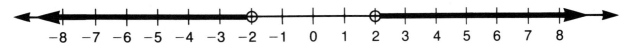

2. $\{x: |x| \leq 5\}$

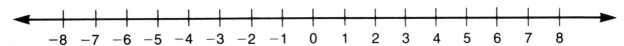

3. $\{x: |x| > 4\}$

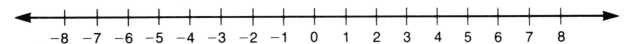

4. $\{x: |x| > 0\}$

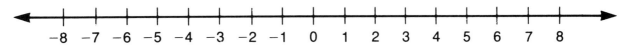

5. $\{x: |x| \leq 0\}$

6. $\{x: |x| - 1 < 3\}$

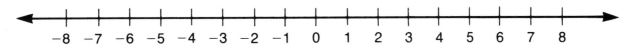

7. $\{x: |x| + 2 \geq 4\}$

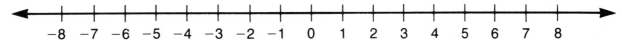

8. $\{x: |x| - 5 < -2\}$

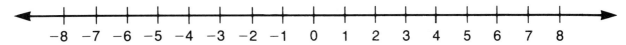

9. $\{x: |x| + 3 < 1\}$

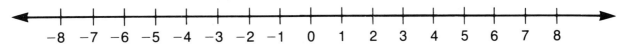

Developing Skills in Algebra   Book C

Absolute Value Inequalities

Name _____

Date _____ Period _____

Graph each set of real numbers.

1. $\{x: |x| - 5 > 1\}$

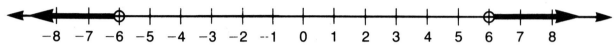

2. $\{x: |x| + 4 \leq 2\}$

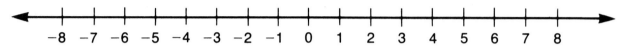

3. $\{x: |x| - 3 > 4\}$

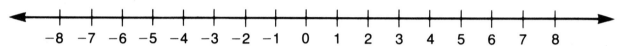

4. $\{x: |x + 2| > 6\}$

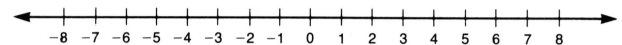

5. $\{x: |x + 3| > 2\}$

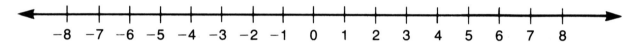

6. $\{x: |x - 4| \leq 3\}$

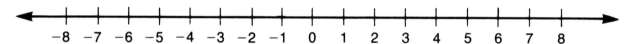

7. $\{x: |x - 1| > 3\}$

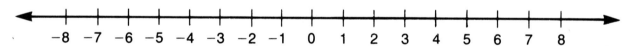

8. $\{x: |x + 2| < 1\}$

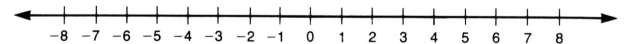

9. $\{x: |x - 3| \geq 1\}$

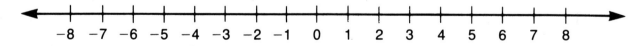

Developing Skills in Algebra Book C

Graphing Linear Inequalities

Name _____

Date _____ Period _____

Graph.

1. $5x - 7y < 11$

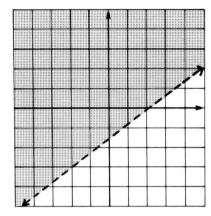

2. $x + 3y \geqslant 10$

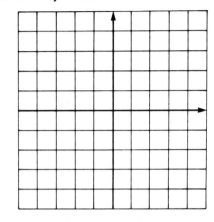

3. $y > x$

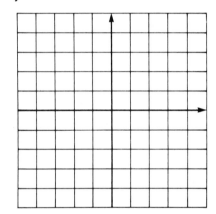

4. $4x + y < 11$

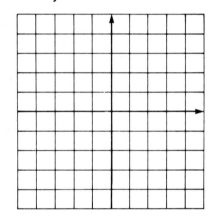

5. $9x - y > 14$

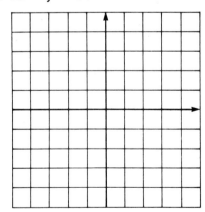

6. $6x + 7y \leqslant -4$

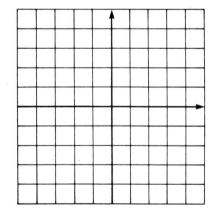

Developing Skills in Algebra   Book C

Graph.

1. $5x - 4y \leqslant -3$

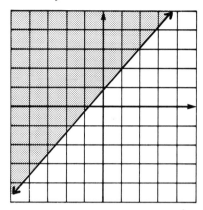

2. $8x + 7y \geqslant -11$

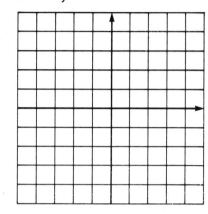

3. $3x + 4y > 11$

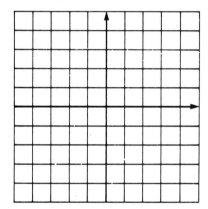

4. $8x - 9y < 5$

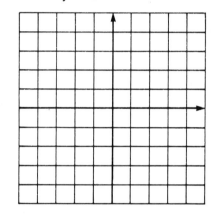

5. $x + 4y < 13$

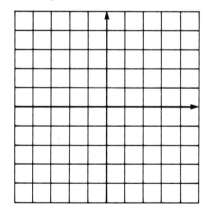

6. $y < -x$

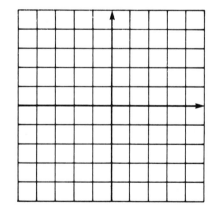

Solving Systems of Inequalities

Name _____

Date _____ Period _____

Graph.

1. $2x - 5y \leq 5$
$2x + y \leq -3$

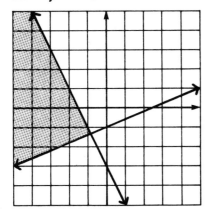

2. $2x + 3y < -6$
$x - y \leq 1$

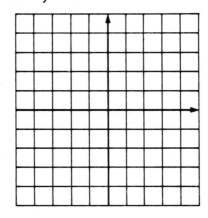

3. $7x - y \geq 26$
$x - y \leq 2$

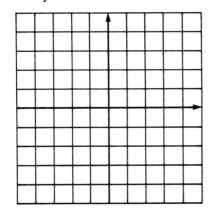

4. $4x + y \geq -23$
$2x - y \leq -7$

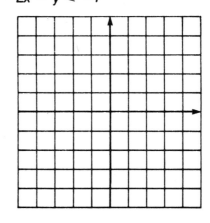

5. $x + y \leq 6$
$x - 2y > 0$

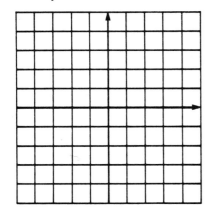

6. $3x - 4y < 17$
$x - 5y \geq 13$

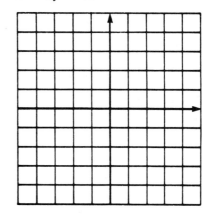

99

Solving Systems of Inequalities

Name _____

Date _____ Period _____

Graph.

1. $5x + 6y > -19$
   $x - 2y > 9$

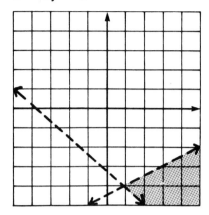

2. $y + 4 \geq 0$
   $4x + 5y \geq 0$

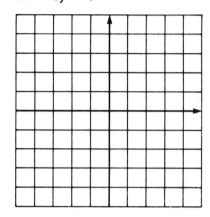

3. $x + y \leq 2$
   $x - 2 \geq 0$

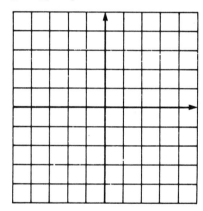

4. $5x - 2y > -11$
   $3y - 2x > 0$

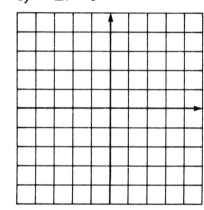

5. $2x - 3y \geq -5$
   $5x - 2y > -7$

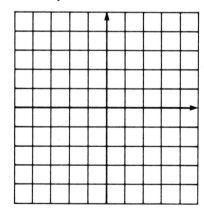

6. $x - 2y \leq 1$
   $2x - y > 4$

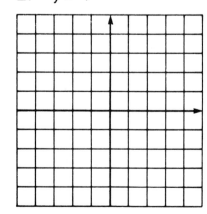

Developing Skills in Algebra Book C

Solving Systems of Inequalities

Name _____

Date _____ Period _____

Graph.

1. $4x + 3y > -5$
   $4x - 3y < 13$

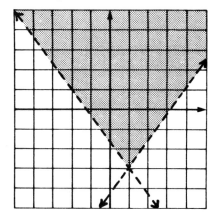

2. $x + y \leq -1$
   $3x - 4y \geq 4$

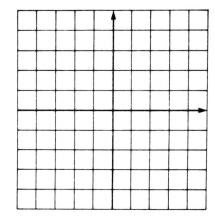

3. $x - 3y > -13$
   $x - y \geq -1$

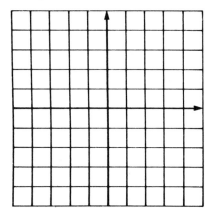

4. $x - 2y < 0$
   $y + 3x \leq 0$

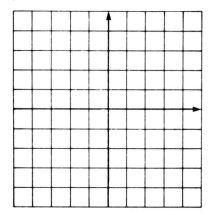

5. $3x + 2y \geq -9$
   $x - y \geq 2$

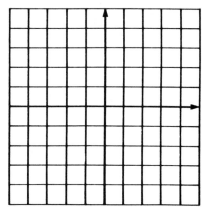

6. $x + 4y < 6$
   $x - y \leq 1$

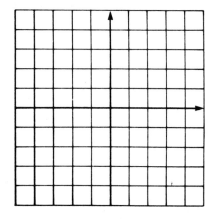

Developing Skills in Algebra   Book C

Solving Systems of Inequalities

Graph.

1. $y > 3x$
$x - y \leq -2$

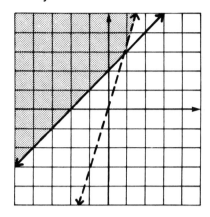

2. $y - 3x \geq 2$
$y \leq x$

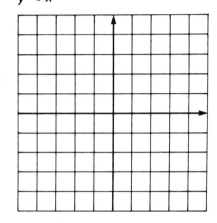

3. $y \leq -x$
$x + 5y > -4$

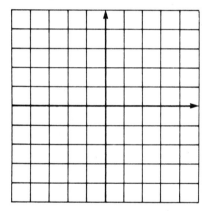

4. $6x - 5y \geq 8$
$3y - x \geq 3$

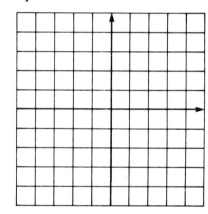

5. $x + 2y < 8$
$5x - 2y \geq 11$

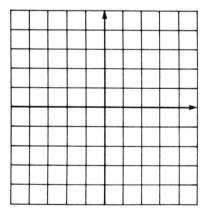

6. $x + y \leq 1$
$x - 9y \leq 41$

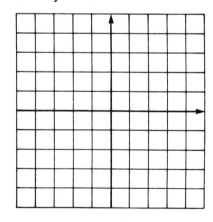

Developing Skills in Algebra   Book C

ANSWERS

Page 1 Ratio

1. 1/2 **2.** 1/3 **3.** 2/5 **4.** 2/3 **5.** 3/8 **6.** 3/4
7. 5/6 **8.** 4/5 **9.** $3x/5y$ **10.** $2y/3x$ **11.** $2x^2/5y^3$
12. $3xy/8$ **13.** $(x-3)/(x+2)$ **14.** $(x+3)/(x-2)$
15. $(x-5)/(x+2)$ **16.** $(x+4)/(x-2)$ **17.** $y/x = 4/9$ **18.** $y/x = 7/10$ **19.** $y/x = 4/5$ **20.** $y/x = 3/4$
21. $y/x = 4/9$ **22.** $y/x = 5/7$ **23.** $y/x = 2/3$
24. $y/x = 3/5$ **25.** $y/x = 1/8$ **26.** $y/x = 3/1$
27. $y/x = -2/1$ **28.** $y/x = 1/2$

Page 2 Ratio

1. 1/4 **2.** 1/3 **3.** 3/7 **4.** 2/3 **5.** 4/7 **6.** 2/5
7. 4/9 **8.** 3/4 **9.** $7x/10y$ **10.** $5y/8$ **11.** $7x^3/12y^2$
12. $4/9x^2y^2$ **13.** $(x-6)/(x+4)$ **14.** $(x-2)/(x+9)$
15. $(x+3)/(x+4)$ **16.** $(x+3)/(x+5)$ **17.** $y/x = 5/7$ **18.** $y/x = 9/8$ **19.** $y/x = 3/5$ **20.** $y/x = 2/5$
21. $y/x = 1/2$ **22.** $y/x = 7/12$ **23.** $y/x = 8/5$
24. $y/x = 2/3$ **25.** $y/x = 8/1$ **26.** $y/x = -1/4$
27. $y/x = 2/5$ **28.** $y/x = -6/1$

Page 3 Ratio

1. 3/5 **2.** 5/6 **3.** 17/12 **4.** 18/13 **5.** 3/2 **6.** 3/2
7. 9/5 **8.** 11/6 **9.** 5 and 25 **10.** 7 and 49
11. 20 and 30 **12.** 28 and 35

Page 4 Ratio

1. 56 and 63 **2.** 80 and 90 **3.** 36 nickels, 45 dimes
4. 12 nickels, 10 quarters **5.** 120 kg sand, 100 kg
cement **6.** 1.25 L **7.** 36 **8.** 12 nickels, 6 quarters
9. 689 **10.** 20

Page 5 Proportion

1. $ad = bc$ **2.** $ad = bc$ **3.** $mq = np$ **4.** $mq = np$ **5.** $x = 5/3$ **6.** $x = 9/4$ **7.** $x = 3/2$ **8.** $x = 10/3$ **9.** $x = 1/2$ **10.** $x = 2/3$ **11.** $x = 29/2$
12. $x = 4$ **13.** $x = 14/5$ **14.** $x = 1/5$ **15.** $x = 17$
16. $x = -1/2$ **17.** $x = 0$ or 3 **18.** $x = 1$ or $-23/43$
19. $x = 5$ or -2 **20.** $x = 4$ or $-3/4$ **21.** $x = 7$
22. $x = 3$ or $-1/4$ **23.** $x = 1$ or 5 **24.** $x = 6$ or -1

Page 6 Proportion

1. $xv = yz$ **2.** $10xs = 21ky$ **3.** $rt = sk$ **4.** $63y = 36x$ **5.** $x = 4$ **6.** $x = 15/4$ **7.** $x = 27/14$ **8.** $x = 11/2$ **9.** $x = -8/3$ **10.** $x = 3/5$ **11.** $x = -10$
12. $x = -13/7$ **13.** $x = 2$ or 2/5 **14.** $x = 7$ **15.** $x = 5$ or 3/2 **16.** $x = 9$ **17.** $x = 8$ or 1 **18.** $x = 2$ or 4 **19.** $x = 8$ or 10 **20.** $x = 5$ or 11 **21.** $x = -1/4$ or 5 **22.** $x = -1/2$ or 7 **23.** $x = -1/9$ or 3 **24.** $x = 9$

Page 7 Proportion

1. 26 gal **2.** 9 cm × 15 cm **3.** 8-1/3 cm, 13-1/3 cm
4. $1250 **5.** 10.5 cm **6.** $x = -17$ **7.** 54
8. $59.50 **9.** 20 and 48 **10.** 12 s

Page 8 Proportion

1. 40 L **2.** 6 cm × 14 cm **3.** 196 cm^2 **4.** $1470
5. 100 km **6.** $x = 55$ **7.** $x = 42$ **8.** $9600
9. width = 10, length = 14 **10.** 15 s

Page 9 Ratio and Proportion

1. 1/3 **2.** 3/13 **3.** $7/3xy^2$ **4.** $(x-14)/(x-7)$
5. $y/x = 7/12$ **6.** $y/x = 10/21$ **7.** $y/x = 5/12$ **8.** $y/x = -9/7$ **9.** $y/x = 1/4$ **10.** $y/x = -2/1$ **11.** 2/3
12. 48 and 42 **13.** $t^6 = r^3s^3$ **14.** $m^2n^3 = p^3q^4$
15. $x = 11$ or 7 **16.** $x = 10$ or -4 **17.** $x = 15$-1/2
18. $x = 66$ **19.** $x = 1$ or 7 **20.** $x = 5$ or 10

Page 10 Ratio and Proportion

1. 2/3 **2.** 1/7 **3.** $2x^2y$ **4.** $(2x-3)/(4x+5)$
5. 7/2 **6.** 1/3 **7.** 5/2 **8.** $-5/11$ **9.** $-1/2$
10. $-4/1$ **11.** 4/5 **12.** 112 and 80 **13.** $kx^2y = k^2xy^2$ **14.** $a^2b^2cd^3 = ab^3cd^3$ **15.** $x = 1/2$ or 7
16. $x = -1/3$ or 2 **17.** $x = 11/7$ **18.** $x = 26$
19. $x = -1/4$ or 3 **20.** $x = -1/3$ or 1

Page 11 Ratio and Proportion

1. 3/5 **2.** 5/3 **3.** $8x^3/y$ **4.** $(5x+3)/(3x+5)$
5. $y/x = 1/2$ **6.** $y/x = 1/6$ **7.** $y/x = 1/2$ **8.** $y/x = 1/2$ **9.** $y/x = 16/3$ **10.** $y/x = -1/17$ **11.** 5/3
12. 9/4 **13.** $a^4b^3 = x^3y^7$ **14.** $m^3n^8 = x^4y^3$ **15.** $x = 0$ or 4 **16.** $x = 2$ or -1 **17.** $x = -22$ **18.** $x = 27$ **19.** $x = 7$ **20.** $x = 9$ or -10

Page 12 Ratio and Proportion

1. 5/7 **2.** 1/4 **3.** $x^2y^2/5$ **4.** $(2x+5)/(x-1)$
5. $y/x = 8/5$ **6.** $y/x = 5/4$ **7.** $y/x = 1/2$ **8.** $y/x = -5/11$ **9.** $y/x = 17/31$ **10.** $y/x = -16/5$ **11.** 66 and 55 **12.** 297 and 243 **13.** $a^4b = r^3s^3t$ **14.** $k^3x^3 = m^3n^3p^3$ **15.** $x = 1/7$ or 3 **16.** $x = 2$ or 11 **17.** $x = -29/19$ **18.** $x = 85$ **19.** $x = 3$ or 12 **20.** $x = 13$

Page 13 Equations with Fractions

1. $x = 12$ **2.** $x = 45$ **3.** $x = 60$ **4.** $x = 120$
5. $x = -42$ **6.** $x = 63$ **7.** $x = 1188$ **8.** $x = 924$
9. $x = 294$ **10.** $x = 560$ **11.** $x = 12$ **12.** $x = -70$ **13.** $x = -48$ **14.** $x = 24$ **15.** $x = -105$
16. $x = -21$ **17.** $x = 5$ **18.** $x = 15$ **19.** $x = 84$
20. $x = 45$ **21.** $x = -21/19$ **22.** $x = -20$ **23.** $x = -21/2$ **24.** $x = -17$ **25.** $x = 22$ **26.** $x = 72/5$

Page 14 Equations with Fractions

1. $x = 21$ **2.** $x = 24$ **3.** $x = 36$ **4.** $x = 63$
5. $x = -1$ **6.** $x = -6$ **7.** $x = 60$ **8.** $x = 30$
9. $x = 70$ **10.** $x = -63$ **11.** $x = 40$ **12.** $x = 99/10$
13. $x = 14$ **14.** $x = 45$ **15.** $x = -20$ **16.** $x = 15$
17. $x = 42$ **18.** $x = -126$ **19.** $x = -24$
20. $x = 60$ **21.** $x = -99/2$ **22.** $x = -15$
23. $x = 84/37$ **24.** $x = -77/38$ **25.** $x = 30/29$
26. $x = -(20/3)$

Page 15 Equations with Fractions

1. $x = 2/3$ **2.** $x = 2/3$ **3.** $x = 1$ **4.** $x = 1$ **5.** $x = 8$ **6.** $x = -27$ **7.** $x = 48$ **8.** $x = 18$ **9.** $x = 20$ **10.** $x = 18$ **11.** $x = 8/3$ **12.** $x = 16/35$
13. $x = 3/2$ **14.** $x = -10$ **15.** $x = 5/2$ **16.** $x = 33/2$ **17.** $x = 6$ **18.** $x = -7$ **19.** $x = 18/23$
20. $x = 11/5$ **21.** $x = 3/8$ **22.** $x = 4/25$ **23.** $x = 9/2$ **24.** $x = 4/3$ **25.** $x = 14$ **26.** $x = 18/33$

Page 16 Equations with Fractions

1. $x = 2$ **2.** $x = 3/2$ **3.** $x = 2/3$ **4.** $x = 6/17$
5. $x = -9$ **6.** $x = -30$ **7.** $x = -80$ **8.** $x = -24$ **9.** $x = -16/3$ **10.** $x = 2$ **11.** $x = -7/4$
12. $x = 20/57$ **13.** $x = 1/3$ **14.** $x = 5/21$ **15.** $x = 36/25$ **16.** $x = 6$ **17.** $x = 3/5$ **18.** $x = -1$ **19.** $x = -(9/4)$ **20.** $x = 3/2$ **21.** $x = 1/2$ **22.** $x = 8/5$
23. $x = 9/16$ **24.** $x = 5/2$ **25.** $x = 27/58$ **26.** $x = 21/44$

Page 17 Equations with Fractions

1. $x = -22$ **2.** $x = 347$ **3.** $x = -5$ **4.** $x = 4$
5. $x = 13$ **6.** $x = -10$ **7.** $x = -(51/2)$ **8.** $x = 27/11$ **9.** $x = 4$ **10.** $x = 6$ **11.** $x = -15/16$
12. $x = 9$ **13.** $x = 18/7$ **14.** $x = 2$ **15.** $x = -3$
16. $x = 6$ **17.** $x = -47/23$ **18.** $x = -7/24$ **19.** $x = 14/15$ **20.** $x = -(3/7)$ **21.** $x = -13/3$ **22.** $x = -(19/5)$ **23.** $x = 3$ **24.** $x = -3$ **25.** $x = -4/3$
26. ϕ

Page 18 Equations with Fractions

1. $x = 24/31$ **2.** $x = 15/43$ **3.** $x = -5$ **4.** $x = -13$ **5.** $x = 7/5$ **6.** $x = -4$ **7.** $x = -43/4$ **8.** $x = 2/27$ **9.** $x = 16/5$ **10.** $x = -21/11$ **11.** $x = 64/5$
12. $x = -3/4$ **13.** $x = 0$ **14.** $x = -4/7$ **15.** $x = -1/16$ **16.** $x = -15/2$ **17.** $x = -23/6$ **18.** $x = 0$
19. $x = -15/2$ **20.** $x = 16/3$ **21.** $x = -17/16$
22. $x = 22/15$ **23.** $x = -13/3$ **24.** $x = -7$ **25.** $x = 21/2$ **26.** $x = 8/13$

Page 19 Equations with Fractions

1. $x = 5$ **2.** $x = 43/2$ **3.** $x = -3/2$ **4.** $x = 1/2$
5. $x = 1/2$ **6.** $x = 11/5$ **7.** $x = 2/7$ **8.** $x = 5/12$
9. $x = 1/5$ **10.** $x = 15$ **11.** $x = 29$ **12.** ϕ
13. $\mathcal{R}$ **14.** $x = -8/5$ **15.** $x = -119/39$
16. $x = -24$

Page 20 Equations with Fractions

1. $x = -1/6$ **2.** $x = 16/5$ **3.** $x = 11/6$ **4.** $x = 13/10$
5. $x = 1/57$ **6.** $x = 75/13$ **7.** $x = 0$ **8.** $x = 2$
9. $x = -2/41$ **10.** $x = -9$ **11.** $x = -20$ **12.** ϕ
13. $\mathcal{R}$ **14.** $x = -19/3$ **15.** $x = 18$ **16.** $x = -4/7$

Page 21 Equations with Fractions

1. $x = 30$ **2.** $x = 1.25$ **3.** $x = 12$ **4.** $x = 0.2$
5. $x = 500$ **6.** $x = -4$ **7.** $x = 3.5$ **8.** $x = 0.7$
9. $x = 2.3$ **10.** $x = 0.65$ **11.** $x = 0.5$ **12.** $x = 0.75$ **13.** $x = -17$ **14.** $x = 50$ **15.** $x = 32$
16. $x = -0.1$

Page 22 Equations with Fractions

1. $x = 0.4$ **2.** $x = 0.23$ **3.** $x = 20$ **4.** $x = 0.2$
5. $x = 50$ **6.** $x = -20$ **7.** $x = 4.5$ **8.** $x = 1.7$
9. $x = 6.25$ **10.** $x = 0.95$ **11.** $x = 0.6$ **12.** $x = 0.95$ **13.** $x = -21$ **14.** $x = 24$ **15.** $x = 19$
16. $x = -0.5$

Page 23 Fractional Equations

1. $x = 1/5$ **2.** $x = -32$ **3.** ϕ **4.** $x = 17/8$ **5.** $x = 2/5$ **6.** $x = 1$ **7.** $y = 9$ **8.** $x = 13/2$ **9.** $y = -1/4$ **10.** $x = -(2/5)$ **11.** $x = -(29/8)$ **12.** $x = 26$ **13.** $x = -23/7$ **14.** $x = -31/2$ **15.** $x = -7$
16. $x = -10$ **17.** $x = -27$ **18.** $x = 32$ **19.** $x = -5/2$ **20.** $x = -5$ **21.** $x = 13/6$ **22.** $x = 47/21$
23. $x = 3/2$ **24.** $x = -3$

Page 24 Fractional Equations

1. $x = 3, x = 6$ **2.** $x = 0, x = 4$ **3.** $x = 3, x = 11/5$
4. $x = -21$ **5.** $x = -1/5, x = 7$ **6.** $x = 8$ **7.** $x = -1/3, x = 2$ **8.** $x = 3$ **9.** $\mathcal{R}, x \ne -1$ **10.** $x = 8$
11. $x = -1/5, x = 1$ **12.** $x = 4$ **13.** $x = 7/4$
14. $x = -3, x = 15$ **15.** $\mathcal{R}, x \ne 1$ **16.** $x = -2/3$
17. $x = -1$ **18.** $x = -7/5, x = 2$ **19.** $x = 6$
20. ϕ **21.** $\mathcal{R}, x \ne -1$ **22.** $x = 8$ **23.** $x = 2$
24. $x = 1/2, x = 3$

Page 25 Fractional Equations

1. $x = 0, x = 4$ **2.** $x = -4, x = 9$ **3.** $x = 7, x = 14$
4. $x = 7, x = 2$ **5.** $x = 15$ **6.** $x = -9, x = 18$
7. $x = 0, x = 10$ **8.** $x = 12$ **9.** $x = 20$ **10.** $\mathcal{R}, x \ne -1$ **11.** $x = 4, x = -2$ **12.** $x = 11, x = 1$
13. $x = 4$ **14.** $x = 10$ **15.** $x = 4, x = 7$ **16.** $x = 5, x = -1$ **17.** $x = 7, x = -1$ **18.** $x = 8$ **19.** $x = 1/5, x = 6$ **20.** $x = 0, x = 2$ **21.** $x = 16$ **22.** $x = 3$
23. $\mathcal{R}, x \ne 3$ **24.** $x = 7$

Page 26 Fractional Equations

1. $x = \pm 1$ **2.** $x = 4, x = 7$ **3.** $x = 0, x = -3$
4. $x = -3/2$ **5.** $x = 0, x = -4$ **6.** $x = 0, x = -7/8$
7. $x = 3$ **8.** $x = 3, x = 1$ **9.** $x = 4, x = 5/7$
10. $x = 3$ **11.** $x = 1/5$ **12.** $x = -1, x = 7$ **13.** $x = 8$ **14.** $x = -1/6$ **15.** ϕ **16.** $x = 2$ **17.** ϕ
18. $x = \pm 4$ **19.** $x = -1$ **20.** $x = 43/4$ **21.** $x = -1/4$

Page 27 Investment Problems

1. $530 at 13%, $1060 at 15% **2.** $340 at 8.5%, $1020 at 12% **3.** $450 at 13%, $1100 at 16% **4.** $725 at 13%, $1675 at 19% **5.** $720 at 6-1/2%, $1120 at 7-1/2%
6. $440 in Alum Savings and Loan, $1260 in Barnum & Bailey Bank **7.** $2290 at 7%, $2710 at 9% **8.** $3050 at 12%, $3950 at 10%

Page 28 Investment Problems

1. $2730 at 12%, $5460 at 18% **2.** $1760 at 8%, $5280 at 11% **3.** $519 at 15%, $1268 at 13% **4.** $904 at 12%, $2212 at 14% **5.** $700 in Coast Federal, $1000 in Rock Bottom Bank **6.** $790 in Safety First Federal, $1500 in Home Savings **7.** $2130 at 8%, $2870 at 12%
8. $3420 at 7%, $5580 at 9%

Page 29 Mixture Problems

1. 5 lb at $1.65, 10 lb at $1.23 **2.** 7 lb at $2.75, 21 lb at $1.50 **3.** 17 lb cashews, 27 lb peanuts **4.** 22 lb walnuts, 37 lb almonds **5.** 12 lb at $6.50, 34 lb at $5.95
6. 15 lb at $4.25, 38 lb at $3.49 **7.** 13 lb at $2.90, 7 lb at $3.15 **8.** 17 lb at $2.75, 13 lb at $3.85

Page 30 Mixture Problems

1. 12 lb at $1.85, 24 lb at $2.34 **2.** 8 lb at $3.25, 24 lb at $2.70 **3.** 13 lb peanuts, 20 lb cashews **4.** 18 lb at $4.95, 7 lb at $3.95 **5.** 26 lb at $5.40, 8 lb at $6.25
6. 23 lb at $5.85, 39 lb at $4.50 **7.** 13 lb at $3.50, 7 lb at $2.95 **8.** 18 lb at $3.15, 12 lb at $4.25

Page 31 Mixture Problems

1. 32 kg **2.** 44 kg **3.** 6 kg of 95%, 9 kg of 75%
4. 12 kg of 35%, 8 kg of 45% **5.** 24 L of 3%, 12 L of 27% **6.** 4 kg of 45%, 11 kg of 75% **7.** 1.5 L water
8. 3 L water **9.** 6 L antifreeze **10.** 12 L sulphuric acid

Page 32 Mixture Problems

1. 12 kg **2.** 45 kg **3.** 10 kg of 63%, 8 kg of 90%
4. 5 kg of 48%, 15 kg of 44% **5.** 18 L of 3%, 15 L of
36% **6.** 9 kg of 56%, 12 kg of 42% **7.** 9 L **8.** 3 L
9. 1 L **10.** 12 L

Page 33 Motion Problems

1. 20 km/h and 30 km/h **2.** 36 km/h and 45 km/h
3. 45 km/h and 50 km/h **4.** 56 km/h and 40 km/h
5. 18 hr and 24 hr **6.** 20 hr and 25 hr **7.** 48 km/h
and 36 km/h **8.** 42 km/h and 56 km/h **9.** 55 km/h and
50 km/h **10** 27 km/h and 30 km/h

Page 34 Motion Problems

1. 42 km/h and 48 km/h **2.** 52 km/h and 78 km/h
3. 25 km/h and 20 km/h **4.** 28 km/h and 35 km/h
5. 9 hr and 6 hr **6.** 10 hr and 12 hr **7.** 80 km/h and
75 km/h **8.** 21 km/h and 28 km/h **9.** 48 km/h and 45
km/h **10.** 30 km/h and 25 km/h

Page 35 Motion Problems

1. 40 km/h and 50 km/h **2.** 33 km/h and 30 km/h
3. 40 km/h and 50 km/h **4.** 30 km/h and 0 km/h
5. 12 hr and 18 hr **6.** 16 hr and 12 hr **7.** 30 km/h
and 50 km/h **8.** 60 km/h and 90 km/h **9.** 66 km/h and
55 km/h **10.** 42 km/h and 35 km/h

Page 36 Motion Problems

1. 25 km/h and 30 km/h **2.** 42 km/h and 36 km/h
3. 14 km/h and 21 km/h **4.** 30 km/h and 55 km/h
5. 6 hr and 9 hr **6.** 10 hr and 14 hr **7.** 60 km/h and
84 km/h **8.** 33 km/h and 66 km/h **9.** 35 km/h and 49
km/h **10.** 39 km/h and 52 km/h

Page 37 Rate of Work Problems

1. 2 hr 55 min **2.** 4-4/9 hr **3.** 4-1/8 hr **4.** 5 hr 4
min **5.** 1 hr 30 min **6.** 1 hr 20 min **7.** 24 hr **8.** 7
hr **9.** 2 hr **10.** 1 hr

Page 38 Rate of Work Problems

1. 3-3/13 hr **2.** 2-8/11 hr **3.** 12 hr **4.** 36 hr **5.** 1
hr 40 min **6.** 3 hr **7.** 12 hr **8.** 7 hr **9.** 4 hr 48 min
10. 4-2/7 hr

Page 39 Rate of Work Problems

1. 2 hr 6 min **2.** 2-2/9 hr **3.** 23 hr 20 min **4.** 7-7/9
hr **5.** 3 hr 28 min **6.** 4 hr 24 min **7.** 5 hr **8.** 10 hr
9. 7 hr 30 min **10.** 11 hr 12 min

Page 40 Rate of Work Problems

1. 3 hr 45 min **2.** 2 hr 24 min **3.** 15 hr **4.** 13-1/8
hr **5.** 1 hr 36 min **6.** 3-1/9 hr **7.** 12 hr **8.** 12 hr
9. 2 hr 12 min **10.** 9 min

Page 41 Equations in Two Variables

1. 5, 3, 1, 7 **2.** −15, −12, −9, −18 **3.** −5, −1,
−9, −15 **4.** 15, 47, −17, −33 **5.** 10, 14, 2, −2
6. 3, 17, −18, −32 **7.** −18, −17, −24, −26 **8.** 7,
1, 16, 22 **9.** 15, 18, −3, 9

Page 42 Equations in Two Variables

1. 19, 40, 47, −16 **2.** 33, 66, 77, 66 **3.** 1, −4, 31,
46 **4.** 34, 48, 62, −15 **5.** −28, −22, −37, −46
6. 57, 102, −105, −132 **7.** −22, −14, −46, −50
8. −19, −25, −4, −34 **9.** −51, −75, 29, 45

Page 43 Equations in Two Variables

1. −5, 13, −41, −47 **2.** 20, 30, 5, 10 **3.** −33,
−37, −1, −17 **4.** −15, 9, 17, −7 **5.** 21, 3, 39, −24
6. −2, 2, −5, 0 **7.** 5, 9, 1, 7 **8.** 2, −8, 12, −13
9. 11, −10, −17, −3

Page 44 Equations in Two Variables

1. 39, 56, −12, −199 **2.** −9, 13, −20, 2 **3.** 18, 4,
32, 11 **4.** −9, −19, 1, −34 **5.** −12, −15, 0, −9
6. 6, 16, −14, −4 **7.** −19, −25, −27, −21 **8.** 15,
−7, 26, 4 **9.** −7, 8, 13, 18

Page 45 Graphing Linear Equations

1. line going through (1, −1), (−3, 4), and (5, 2) **2.** line
going through (−1, −5), (0, 2), and (1, 1) **3.** line going
through (0, 0), (−4, 2), and (2, −1) **4.** line going through
(0, −2), (3, 4), and (−2, −6) **5.** line going through (0, 2),
(−3, 4), and (3, 0) **6.** line going through (0, 1), (−1, 4),
and (2, −5)

Page 46 Graphing Linear Equations

1. line going through (1, −2), (−1, 1), and (−3, 4)
2. line going through (0, −4), (1, −2), and (2, 0) **3.** line
going through (0, 2), (−3, 0), and (3, 4) **4.** line going
through (−5, 4), (−2, 0), and (1, −4) **5.** line going
through (0, 0), (1, −1), and (2, −2) **6.** line going through
(0, 2), (−5, 0), and (5, 4)

Page 47 Graphing Linear Equations

1. line going through (−4, −1), (−1, 1), and (2, 3)
2. line going through (0, −3), (4, −4), and (−4, −2)
3. line going through (0, −1), (−4, 1), and (4, −3)
4. line going through (0, 3), (−4, 0), and (4, 6) **5.** line
going through (0, 1), (3, 3), and (−3, −1) **6.** line going
through (0, 2), (3, 1), and (−3, 3)

Page 48 Graphing Linear Equations

1. line going through (1, −1), (4, −2), and (−2, 0)
2. line going through (0, 1), (2, −3), and (−1, 3) **3.** line
going through (−1, −3), (1, −4), and (−3, −2) **4.** line
going through (0, −1), (4, 2), and (−4, −4) **5.** line going
through (0, 1), (5, 5), and (−5, −3) **6.** line going through
(0, −2), (4, −4), and (−4, 0)

Page 49 Graphing in the Coordinate Plane

1. $m = -1$ **2.** $m = 4$ **3.** $m = 0$ **4.** $m = 2/3$
5. $m = -3/2$ **6.** no slope **7.** $m = -2$ **8.** $m = -1/4$

Page 50 Graphing in the Coordinate Plane

1. $m = 1$ **2.** no slope **3.** $m = -3/2$ **4.** $m = 3$
5. $m = 0$ **6.** $m = -1/4$ **7.** $m = 2$ **8.** $m = -(2/3)$

Page 51 Slope of a Line

1. 1/5 **2.** −1 **3.** −3 **4.** 4 **5.** 1/4 **6.** no slope
7. 1 **8.** −(5/2) **9.** no slope **10.** 7/5 **11.** 0
12. −5 **13.** 3/10 **14.** −1 **15.** −(9/2) **16.** 0
17.   **18.**

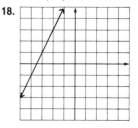

19.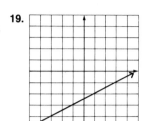

20.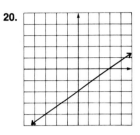

31.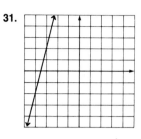

32.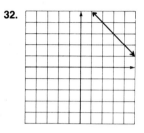

21.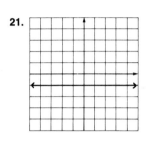

22.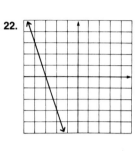

23.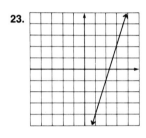

24.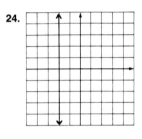

17.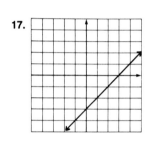

18.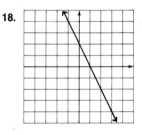

25.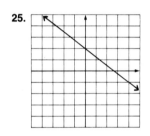

26.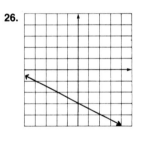

19.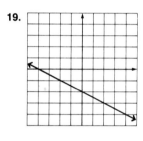

20.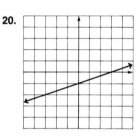

27.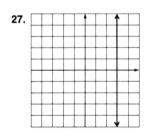

28.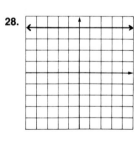

21.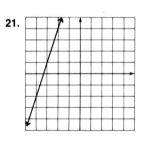

22.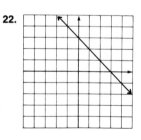

29.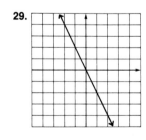

30.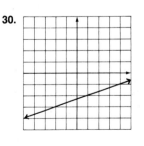

23.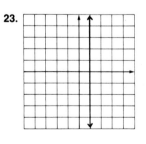

24.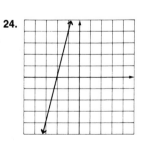

25.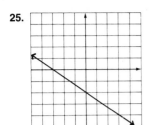

26.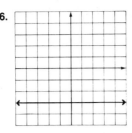

27.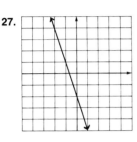

28.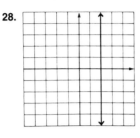

29.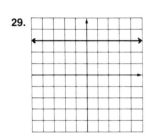

30.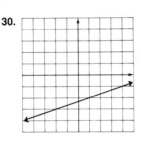

31.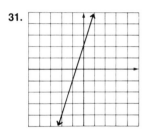

32.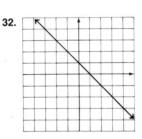

30. $3x + 6y = 4$ **31.** $2x + y = -3$ **32.** $9x + 6y = 10$
33. $4y = 3$ **34.** $9x - 3y = -2$

Page 54 Equations in Two Variables

1. $y = -4x + 2, m = -4, b = 2$ **2.** $y = -3x + 1, m = -3, b = 1$ **3.** $y = -(1/2)x + 5, m = -1/2, b = 5$ **4.** $y = -(1/7)x + 2, m = -1/7, b = 2$ **5.** $y = 3x - 2, m = 3, b = -2$ **6.** $y = 2x - 4, m = 2, b = -4$ **7.** $y = (1/2)x - 5, m = 1/2, b = -5$ **8.** $y = (1/3)x - 5, m = 1/3, b = -5$ **9.** $y = -(3/2)x + 6, m = -3/2, b = 6$ **10.** $y = -(2/5)x + 4, m = -2/5, b = 4$ **11.** $y = (4/7)x - 3, m = 4/7, b = -3$ **12.** $y = (3/4)x - 1, m = 3/4, b = -1$ **13.** $y = -(2/3)x + (10/3), m = -(2/3), b = 10/3$ **14.** $y = -(4/5)x + (11/5), m = -4/5, b = 11/5$ **15.** $y = (7/8)x - (9/8), m = 7/8, b = -9/8$ **16.** $y = (5/7)x - (3/7), m = 5/7, b = -3/7$ **17.** $y = -(3/2)x + (11/2), m = -3/2, b = 11/2$ **18.** $y = (9/4)x - (1/2), m = 9/4, b = -1/2$ **19.** $y = (5/8)x - (3/2), m = 5/8, b = -3/2$ **20.** $y = (3/10)x - (8/5), m = 3/10, b = -8/5$
21. $2x - y = -3$ **22.** $3x - y = 1$ **23.** $2x - 3y = 6$ **24.** $x - 2y = -8$ **25.** $x + y = 0$ **26.** $y = -2$ **27.** $x + 2y = -8$ **28.** $15x + 3y = 2$ **29.** $12x - 3y = -1$ **30.** $3x - 2y = 0$ **31.** $3x + 4y = 5$ **32.** $3x - 12y = 8$ **33.** $4x + 12y = 15$ **34.** $4x + y = -1$

Page 55 Equations in Two Variables

1. $2x - y = 5$ **2.** $3x + y = 14$ **3.** $x + y = 4$ **4.** $x - y = -2$ **5.** $3x - y = 0$ **6.** $2x + y = -1$ **7.** $x - 2y = -4$ **8.** $2x - 3y = 0$ **9.** $y = -4$ **10.** $5x + 2y = -1$ **11.** $3x + 4y = -12$ **12.** $x + 3y - 3$ **13.** $5x - y = -11$ **14.** $5x - 3y = -23$ **15.** $x - 3y = 8$ **16.** $x - 4y = 3$ **17.** $4x + 3y = 4$ **18.** $y = -5$ **19.** $x - 5y = -17$ **20.** $x - 3y = -13$ **21.** $x - 2y = -1$ **22.** $x + 4y = 17$ **23.** $x = 3$ **24.** $2x - y = 7$ **25.** $2x - y = 0$ **26.** $x - 2y = -4$ **27.** $y = -3$ **28.** $4x - 3y = -33$ **29.** $2x - y = 7$ **30.** $5x + 2y = 0$ **31.** $x - 3y = 5$ **32.** $x - 2y = -3$ **33.** $2x - y = 5$ **34.** $2x - y = 8$

Page 56 Equations in Two Variables

1. $x - y = 0$ **2.** $x - y = 1$ **3.** $3x - y = 0$ **4.** $4x - y = 0$ **5.** $x + y = -1$ **6.** $y = -2$ **7.** $2x - y = 1$ **8.** $3x + y = -7$ **9.** $x - 3y = 1$ **10.** $x - 2y = -8$ **11.** $y = -2$ **12.** $3x + 4y = -2$ **13.** $2x + 3y = -9$ **14.** $x - 5y = 16$ **15.** $3x - 2y = -4$ **16.** $5x - 3y = 9$ **17.** $4x - 3y = -2$ **18.** $6x - 5y = 29$ **19.** $x + 2y = -3$ **20.** $3x + 2y = 0$ **21.** $x - y = -2$ **22.** $x + 3y = 11$ **23.** $2x + y = 5$ **24.** $x = 4$ **25.** $3x - 2y = 13$ **26.** $x - 2y = -8$ **27.** $x + 4y = 0$ **28.** $y = -3$ **29.** $2x - y = 2$ **30.** $x = -2$ **31.** $x = 5$ **32.** $x - y = 2$ **33.** $3x + y = 9$ **34.** $2x - 3y = 4$

Page 57 Equations in Two Variables

See student graphs.

1. $m = -1, b = 5$ **2.** $m = -1, b = 3$ **3.** $m = 1, b = -1$ **4.** $m = 1, b = -4$ **5.** $m = -2, b = 2$ **6.** $m = -3, b = 3$ **7.** $m = 2/3, b = -2$ **8.** $m = 3/2, b = -3$ **9.** $m -4/3, b = 3$ **10.** $m = -2/3, b = 4$ **11.** $m = 1/3, b = -4$ **12.** $m = 3/5, b = -2$ **13.** $m = 2/5, b = -3$ **14.** $m = 3/4, b = -4$ **15.** $m = 3/5, b = 2$ **16.** $m = 1/3, b = 3$ **17.** $m = 1/3, b = 2$ **18.** $m = 5/3, b = 5$

Page 53 Equations in Two Variables

1. $y = -3x + 5, m = -3, b = 5$ **2.** $y = -2x + 3, m = -2, b = 3$ **3.** $y = -(1/3)x + 3, m = -1/3, b = 3$ **4.** $y = -(1/2)x + 4, m = -1/2, b = 4$ **5.** $y = 4x - 1, m = 4, b = -1$ **6.** $y = 5x - 3, m = 5, b = -3$ **7.** $y = (1/4)x - 4, m = 1/4, b = -4$ **8.** $y = (1/5)x - 2, m = 1/5, b = -2$ **9.** $y = -(2/3)x + 2, m = -2/3, b = 2$ **10.** $y = -(3/2)x + 5, m = -3/2, b = 5$ **11.** $y = (5/4)x - 2, m = 5/4, b = -2$ **12.** $y = (7/5)x - 3, m = 7/5, b = -3$ **13.** $y = -(3/2)x + (5/2), m = -3/2, b = 5/2$ **14.** $y = -(7/5)x + (2/5), m = -7/5, b = 2/5$ **15.** $y = (4/7)x - (10/7), m = 4/7, b = -10/7$ **16.** $y = (6/7)x - (9/7), m = 6/7, b = 9/7$ **17.** $y = -(5/2)x + (13/2), m = -5/2, b = 13/2$ **18.** $y = (2/3)x - (4/3), m = 2/3, b = -4/3$ **19.** $y = (1/2)x - 5/4, m = 1/2, b = -5/4$ **20.** $y = (2/5)x - 13/5, m = 2/5, b = -13/5$
21. $4x - y = -1$ **22.** $2x - y = 2$ **23.** $x - 2y = 6$ **24.** $2x - 3y = 3$ **25.** $3x - 2y = -5$ **26.** $3x + 5y = 0$ **27.** $x - y = 4$ **28.** $y = 3$ **29.** $3x - 5y = 0$

Page 58 Equations in Two Variables

See student graphs.

1. $m = -1, b = 2$ **2.** $m = -1, b = 4$ **3.** $m = 1, b = -3$ **4.** $m = 1, b = -5$ **5.** $m = -3, b = 4$ **6.** $m = -2, b = 3$ **7.** $m = 3/2, b = -1$ **8.** $m = 2/3, b = -2$ **9.** $m = -5/2, b = 5$ **10.** $m = 3/4, b = -3$ **11.** $m = 1/4, b = -2$ **12.** $m = 2/5, b = -2$ **13.** $m = -3/2, b = 5$ **14.** $m = -2, b = -4$ **15.** $m = -2/3, b = -2$ **16.** $m = 1/4, b = 2$ **17.** $m = 5/2, b = -2$ **18.** $m = -4/3, b = 2$

Page 59 Solving Equations with Two Variables

See student graphs.

1. $(1, 2)$ **2.** $(0, 1)$ **3.** $(2, 1)$ **4.** $(0, -1)$ **5.** $(3, -2)$ **6.** $(-1, 2)$ **7.** $(0, -2)$ **8.** $(-1, 1)$ **9.** $(2, 2)$ **10.** ϕ **11.** $(-1, -2)$ **12.** $(3, 3)$ **13.** $(1, 3)$ **14.** $\{(x, y) : y = 2x + 1\}$ **15.** ϕ **16.** $(-2, 2)$ **17.** $(-1, 2)$ **18.** $(2, -1)$ **19.** ϕ **20.** $(1, 4)$ **21.** $\{(x, y) : 2x + 3y = 8\}$ **22.** $(2, 1)$ **23.** ϕ **24.** $(-3, -1)$

Page 60 Solving Equations with Two Variables

See student graphs.

1. $(0, 2)$ **2.** $(-1, 0)$ **3.** $(3, 2)$ **4.** $(2, -1)$ **5.** $(2, 3)$ **6.** $(-1, -2)$ **7.** ϕ **8.** $(-1, 2)$ **9.** $\{(x, y) : 2x - y = -2\}$ **10.** $(2, 2)$ **11.** ϕ **12.** $(-2, -1)$ **13.** $(2, 4)$ **14.** ϕ **15.** $(-3, -2)$ **16.** $(2, 4)$ **17.** $\{(x, y) : 4x - 3y = -5\}$ **18.** $(2, 3)$ **19.** $(3, 3)$ **20.** ϕ **21.** $(-1, 2)$ **22.** $(-2, -3)$ **23.** $(-2, 3)$ **24.** $(1, 3)$

Page 61 Solving Equations with Two Variables

1. $(4, 1)$ **2.** $(-1, 3)$ **3.** $(8, 3)$ **4.** $(7, 2)$ **5.** $(12, 9)$ **6.** $(1, -5)$ **7.** $(3, 4)$ **8.** $(2, 2)$ **9.** $(1, 8)$ **10.** $(-4, 3)$ **11.** $(6, 3)$ **12.** $(4, -5)$ **13.** $(-3, -4)$ **14.** $(6, -5)$ **15.** $(8, -10)$ 16. $(1/2, -3)$ **17.** $(-2, -1/2)$ **18.** $(1/3, 3)$ **19.** $(2, -1)$ **20.** $(2, -3)$ **21.** $(1/2, 0)$ **22.** $(4, -1/2)$ **23.** $(1/4, 1/5)$ **24.** $(3/4, 1/4)$

Page 62 Solving Equations with Two Variables

1. $(8, 1)$ **2.** $(2, 1)$ **3.** $(10, 12)$ **4.** $(3, 1)$ **5.** $(-2, -8)$ **6.** $(-2, -12)$ **7.** $(1, 2)$ **8.** $(2, 1)$ **9.** $(-1, -15)$ **10.** $(2, 0)$ **11.** $(-2, -11)$ **12.** $(-4, -2)$ **13.** $(-1, -2)$ **14.** $(2, 2)$ **15.** $(-2, -10)$ **16.** $(6, -1/3)$ **17.** $(-1/4, -13/4)$ **18.** $(29, 5)$ **19.** $(2, -1)$ **20.** $(13/5, 1/5)$ **21.** $(13/4, 1)$ **22.** $(2, 5/3)$ **23.** $(1/2, -1/5)$ **24.** $(1, 3/2)$

Page 63 Solving Equations with Two Variables

1. $(9, 1)$ **2.** $(10, 3)$ **3.** $(1, 2)$ **4.** $(-1, -2)$ **5.** $\{(x, y) : 3x + y = 5\}$ **6.** $(3, -4)$ **7.** $(-2, 1)$ **8.** $(2, 5)$ **9.** $(-1, 1)$ **10.** $\{(x, y) : 2x - 3y = 4\}$ **11.** ϕ **12.** $(-3, 1)$ **13.** $(2, -3)$ **14.** $(-4, -2)$ **15.** $(-4, 2)$ **16.** ϕ **17.** $(5, -3)$ **18.** $(1, 5)$ **19.** $(-3, 7)$ **20.** $(3, -2)$ **21.** $\{(x, y) : 3x + y = 13\}$ **22.** $(1, -6)$ **23.** $(-3, -1)$ **24.** $(-3, 4)$

Page 64 Solving Equations with Two Variables

1. $(1, 3)$ **2.** $(3, -5)$ **3.** $(2, -3)$ **4.** $(-4, -3)$ **5.** $(-1, -2)$ **6.** $(-2, -4)$ **7.** $(2, 5)$ **8.** $(-3, 5)$ **9.** $(5, -1)$ **10.** ϕ **11.** ϕ **12.** $(-4, 3)$ **13.** $(-1, -3)$ **14.** $(-3, 5)$ **15.** $(2, -4)$ **16.** $\{(x, y) : 2x - 5y = 9\}$ **17.** $(4, -3)$ **18.** ϕ **19.** $(2, 4)$ **20.** $(1, 4)$ **21.** ϕ **22.** $(-3, 1)$ **23.** $(-5, 7)$ **24.** $(0, -2)$

Page 65 Solving Equations with Two Variables

1. $(2, -1)$ **2.** $(-2, -4)$ **3.** $\{(x, y) : 7x - 4y = 15\}$ **4.** $(5, -3)$ **5.** $(-3, 1)$ **6.** $(-6, 1)$ **7.** $(-2, -2)$ **8.** ϕ **9.** $(0, 5)$ **10.** $(1, 4)$ **11.** $(3, 4)$ **12.** $(-3, 0)$ **13.** $\{(x, y) : 2x - 6y = 1\}$ **14.** $\{(x, y) : 2x - 5y = 3\}$ **15.** ϕ **16.** $(-1/2, 3/7)$ **17.** $(2/3, 1/2)$ **18.** ϕ **19.** $(-4, 3)$ **20.** $(2, 7)$ **21.** $(2/5, -1)$ **22.** ϕ **23.** ϕ **24.** $(1/3, 1/2)$

Page 66 Solving Equations with Two Variables

1. $(2, -1)$ **2.** $(-3, 2)$ **3.** $(3, -3)$ **4.** ϕ **5.** $\{(x, y) : 4x + 3y = 7\}$ **6.** $(1, 4)$ **7.** $(-5, 0)$ **8.** $\{(x, y) : 6x - 4y = -6\}$ **9.** ϕ **10.** $(2, -1)$ **11.** $(-4, 1)$ **12.** $(-1, -1)$ **13.** $(5, 2)$ **14.** ϕ **15.** $\{(x, y) : 3x - 2y = 2\}$ **16.** $\{(x, y) : 4x - y = -2\}$ **17.** ϕ **18.** $(0, -2)$ **19.** $(1/2, 1/3)$ **20.** $(2, 2/5)$ **21.** $(4, -1/2)$ **22.** $(2, -1)$ **23.** $(6, 3)$ **24.** $(1/2, -1/3)$

Page 67 Number Problems

1. 3 and 15 **2.** 3 and 23 **3.** 10 and 24 **4.** 11 and 17 **5.** 6 and 36 **6.** 29 and 51 **7.** 10 and 25 **8.** 6 and 14 **9.** 4 and 7 **10.** 4 and 10

Page 68 Number Problems

1. 14 and 22 **2.** 12 and 15 **3.** 26 and 31 **4.** 46 and 62 **5.** 11 and 27 **6.** 39 and 86 **7.** 43 and 25 **8.** 44 and 21 **9.** 1/8 and 27/8 **10.** -12 and 1

Page 69 Perimeter Problems

1. 5 cm × 11 cm **2.** 13 cm × 15 cm **3.** 6 m × 15 m **4.** 10 cm × 21 cm **5.** 12 cm × 26 cm **6.** 8 m × 25 m **7.** 12 m × 30 m **8.** 8 m × 18 m **9.** 8 cm × 21 cm **10.** 12 cm × 20 cm

Page 70 Perimeter Problems

1. 17 cm × 5 cm **2.** 23 cm × 14 cm **3.** 49 m × 12 m **4.** 41 m × 8 m **5.** 30 cm × 24 cm **6.** 7 m × 5 m **7.** 17 m × 1.5 m **8.** 7 cm × 4 cm **9.** 11 m × 4 m **10.** 6 cm × 4 cm

Page 71 Age Problems

1. 24 yr and 5 yr **2.** 14 yr and 43 yr **3.** 20 yr and 60 yr **4.** 10 yr and 40 yr **5.** 5 yr and 9 yr **6.** 8 yr and 3 yr **7.** 9 yr and 19 yr **8.** 7 yr and 15 yr **9.** 11 yr and 20 yr **10.** 10 yr and 18 yr

Page 72 Age Problems

1. 10 yr and 39 yr **2.** 12 yr and 35 yr **3.** 21 yr and 50 yr **4.** 12 yr and 42 yr **5.** 10 yr and 12 yr **6.** 5 yr and 16 yr **7.** 15 yr and 21 yr **8.** 5 yr and 19 yr **9.** 20 yr and 26 yr **10.** 12 yr and 16 yr

Page 73 Digit Problems

1. 56 **2.** 32 **3.** 45 **4.** 81 **5.** 64 **6.** 15 **7.** 72 **8.** 15 **9.** 26 **10.** 94

Page 74 Digit Problems

1. 35 **2.** 47 **3.** 18 **4.** 64 **5.** 23 **6.** 53 **7.** 86 **8.** 49 **9.** 29 **10.** 74

Page 75 Money Problems

1. $1.15 and $2.45 **2.** $2.25 and $3.85 **3.** $0.26 and $0.32 **4.** $0.79 and $0.69 **5.** $49.98 and $24.49 **6.** $59.95 and $16.49 **7.** $16.85 and $8.95 **8.** $25.49 and $10.98 **9.** $4.65 and $5.35 **10.** $6.50 and $4.35

Page 76 Money Problems

1. $1.25 and $1.75 **2.** $0.90 and $1.35 **3.** $0.29 and $0.36 **4.** $0.89 and $0.45 **5.** $79.95 and $39.00 **6.** $119.95 and $29.98 **7.** $35.00 and $21.00 **8.** $24.90 and $7.50 **9.** $2.49 and $3.15 **10.** $18.00 and $8.50

Page 77 Motion Problems

1. rate in still water: 8 km/h, current: 2 km/h **2.** rate in still water: 12 km/h, current: 3 km/h **3.** rate in still water: 9 km/h, current: 3 km/h **4.** rate in still water: 10 km/h, current: 2 km/h **5.** rate in still air: 140 km/h, wind: 40 km/h **6.** rate in still air: 156 km/h, wind: 39 km/h **7.** rate in still air: 525 km/h, wind: 75 km/h **8.** rate in still air: 510 km/h, wind: 90 km/h

Page 78 Motion Problems

1. rate in still water: 7 km/h, current: 2 km/h **2.** rate in still water: 7.5 km/h, current: 2.5 km/h **3.** rate in still water: 3.5 km/h, current: 0.5 km/h **4.** rate in still water: 5.5 km/h, current: 1.5 km/h **5.** rate in still air: 80 km/h, wind: 30 km/h **6.** rate in still air: 120 km/h, wind: 20 km/h **7.** rate in still air: 540 km/h, wind: 60 km/h **8.** rate in still air: 500 km/h, wind: 100 km/h

Page 79 Temperature Problems

1. $20°$ C, $68°$ F **2.** $50°$ C, $122°$ F **3.** $-10°$ C, $14°$ F **4.** $-5°$ C, $23°$ F **5.** $25°$ C, $77°$ F **6.** $5°$ C, $41°$ F **7.** $70°$ C, $158°$ F **8.** $15°$ C, $59°$ F

Page 80 Temperature Problems

1. $30°$ C, $86°$ F **2.** $90°$ C, $194°$ F **3.** $25°$ C, $77°$ F **4.** $-5°$ C, $23°$ F **5.** $45°$ C, $113°$ F **6.** $100°$ C, $212°$ F **7.** $65°$ C, $149°$ F **8.** $85°$ C, $185°$ F

Page 81 Mixture Problems

1. $1.05: 18 lb, $1.35: 12 lb **2.** $2.25: 21 lb, $3.25: 14 lb **3.** $3.75: 16 lb, $4.35: 24 lb **4.** apricots: 16 lb, prunes: 9 lb **5.** 12%: 10 L, 16%: 30 L **6.** 3%: 10 L, 18%: 5 L **7.** pure copper: 6 kg, alloy: 30 kg **8.** pure tin: 4 kg, alloy: 28 kg

Page 82 Mixture Problems

1. $1.25: 27 lb, $1.50: 18 lb **2.** $2.90: 33 lb, $4.60: 18 lb **3.** $2.95: 16 lb, $3.50: 28 lb **4.** $5.75: 12 lb, $3.80: 40 lb **5.** 25%: 8 L, 18%: 20 L **6.** 2%: 4 L, 12%: 6 L **7.** 12%: 10 kg, 32%: 34 kg **8.** pure tin: 34 kg, alloy: 150 kg

Page 83 Miscellaneous Word Problems

1. 32 and 19 **2.** 15 cm $\times$ 19 cm **3.** 8 yr and 33 yr **4.** -2 and -1 **5.** -29 and -25 **6.** 27 **7.** $2.19 and $3.00 **8.** rate in still water: 3.5 km/h, current: 0.5 km/h **9.** $-20°$ C, $-4°$ F **10.** $0.95: 12 kg, $1.85: 15 kg

Page 84 Miscellaneous Word Problems

1. 65 and 11 **2.** 21 cm $\times$ 36 cm **3.** 12 yr and 37 yr **4.** 2 and -2 **5.** -4 and -1 **6.** 85 **7.** $6.50 and $8.40 **8.** rate in still water: 9 km/h, current: 7 km/h **9.** $60°$ C, $140°$ F **10.** $2.95: 12.5 kg, $6.25: 20.5 kg

Page 85 Miscellaneous Word Problems

1. 108 and -14 **2.** 16 m $\times$ 50 m **3.** 7 yr and 35 yr **4.** 0 and -9 **5.** -5 and -10 **6.** 98 **7.** oranges: 19¢, apples: 29¢ **8.** rate in still air: 91 km/h, wind: 11 km/h **9.** $50°$ C, $122°$ F **10.** 9%: 12 L, 30%: 9 L

Page 86 Miscellaneous Word Problems

1. 115 and -75 **2.** 6 cm $\times$ 39 cm **3.** 25 yr and 50 yr **4.** 2 and 5 **5.** 7 and -11 **6.** 72 **7.** avocados: 49¢, tomatoes: 36¢ **8.** rate in still air: 123 km/h, wind: 41 km/h **9.** $15°$ C, $59°$ F **10.** pure copper: 12 kg, alloy: 120 kg

Page 87 Solving Inequalities

1. $x < 3$ **2.** $x > 5$ **3.** $x > 5$ **4.** $x < 8$ **5.** $x < 17$ **6.** $x > 22$ **7.** $x < 6$ **8.** $x \geq 6$ **9.** $x > 7$ **10.** $x < 6$ **11.** $x > -7$ **12.** $x < -6$ **13.** $x < -7$ **14.** $x > 0$ **15.** $x \leq -4$ **16.** $x < -10$ **17.** $x < 3$ **18.** $x > 5$ **19.** $x > 3$ **20.** $x < 7$ **21.** $x < 21$ **22.** $x > 22$ **23.** $x < 4$ **24.** $x \geq 5/2$ **25.** $x > 5$ **26.** $x < 4$ **27.** $x > -5$ **28.** $x < -2$ **29.** $x \leq -2$ **30.** $x > -1$ **31.** $x < -7$ **32.** $x < 6$

Page 88 Solving Inequalities

1. $x < 2$ **2.** $x < 4$ **3.** $x > 3$ **4.** $x > -21$ **5.** $x < 21$ **6.** $x < -4$ **7.** $x < 8$ **8.** $x < 10$ **9.** $x \geq 7$ **10.** $x > 10$ **11.** $x > -9$ **12.** $x > 4$ **13.** $x < -8$ **14.** $x \geq -13$ **15.** $x < -9$ **16.** $x < -4$ **17.** $x > 4$ **18.** $x > 3$ **19.** $x < 9$ **20.** $x < -27$ **21.** $x > 45$ **22.** $x \geq 40$ **23.** $x > 11$ **24.** $x > 2$ **25.** $x \leq 9$ **26.** $x < 5$ **27.** $x > -14$ **28.** $x < -14$ **29.** $x > -6$ **30.** $x > -9$ **31.** $x < -10$ **32.** $x \leq -9$

Page 89 Solving Inequalities

1. $x > -3$ **2.** $x < 8$ **3.** $x < 9$ **4.** $x > -8$ **5.** $x > 5$ **6.** $x > 1$ **7.** $x \geq 2$ **8.** $x < 6$ **9.** $x < -13$ **10.** $x > -9$ **11.** $x < 2$ **12.** $x \geq 9$ **13.** $x < -2$ **14.** $x > -2$ **15.** $x > -3$ **16.** $x < -5$ **17.** $x \geq 8$ **18.** $x \leq 3$ **19.** $x < -3$ **20.** $x > -6$ **21.** $x > -2$ **22.** $x < 3$ **23.** $x \geq 16/7$ **24.** $x > -10$ **25.** $x > 6$ **26.** $x < -5$ **27.** $x > -3$ **28.** $x \leq 3$ **29.** $x < -3$ **30.** $x < -2$ **31.** $x \geq 7$ **32.** $x < 7$

Page 90 Solving Inequalities

1. $x > -2$ **2.** $x < 4$ **3.** $x < 4$ **4.** $x > -3$ **5.** $x \geq 5$ **6.** $x > 5$ **7.** $x > 4$ **8.** $x < -4$ **9.** $x < -5$ **10.** $x > -10$ **11.** $x < 7$ **12.** $x \geq 8$ **13.** $x < -1$ **14.** $x > -2$ **15.** $x > -51/35$ **16.** $x < -19/24$ **17.** $x \geq 6$ **18.** $x < 3$ **19.** $x < -3$ **20.** $x > -62/21$ **21.** $x > -5/2$ **22.** $x \leq 1$ **23.** $x \geq 4$ **24.** $x > -5/2$ **25.** $x > 10/3$ **26.** $x < 3$ **27.** $x > -7/9$ **28.** $x < 3$ **29.** $x < -4$ **30.** $x > 2$ **31.** $x \leq -1$ **32.** $x > -2$

Page 91 Solving Absolute Value Equations

1. $x = \pm 5$ **2.** $x = \pm 7$ **3.** $x = \pm 10$ **4.** $x = \pm 25$ **5.** $x = \pm 12$ **6.** $x = \pm 9$ **7.** $x = 0$ **8.** ϕ **9.** $x = \pm 1$ **10.** $x = \pm 8$ **11.** $x = \pm 13$ **12.** $x = \pm 17$ **13.** $x = \pm 2$ **14.** $x = \pm 7$ **15.** $x = \pm 24$ **16.** $x = \pm 31$ **17.** $x = \pm 21$ **18.** $x = \pm 25$ **19.** $x = \pm 25$ **20.** $x = \pm 35$ **21.** ϕ **22.** $x = \pm 12$ **23.** $x = 5$ or -9 **24.** $x = 7$ or -17 **25.** ϕ **26.** $x = \pm 10$ **27.** $x = 9$ or -17 **28.** $x = 18$ or -32 **29.** $x = 11$ or 7 **30.** $x = 23$ or 3 **31.** $x = 8$ or -14 **32.** $x = 6$ or -34

Page 92 Solving Absolute Value Equations

1. $x = \pm 8$ **2.** $x = \pm 12$ **3.** $x = \pm 14$ **4.** $x = \pm 22$ **5.** $x = \pm 13$ **6.** $x = \pm 29$ **7.** ϕ **8.** $x = \pm 24$ **9.** $x = \pm 4$ **10.** $x = \pm 9$ **11.** $x = \pm 12$ **12.** $x = \pm 14$ **13.** $x = \pm 12$ **14.** $x = \pm 10$ **15.** $x = \pm 20$ **16.** $x = \pm 44$ **17.** $x = \pm 40$ **18.** $x = \pm 13$ **19.** $x = \pm 28$ **20.** $x = \pm 34$ **21.** $x = \pm 4$ **22.** $x = \pm 14$ **23.** $x = \pm 32$ **24.** $x = \pm 17$ **25.** $x = 7$ or -13 **26.** ϕ **27.** $x = 9$ or -17 **28.** $x = 18$ or -32 **29.** $x = 9$ or -19 **30.** $x = 18$ or -30 **31.** $x = 10$ or 4 **32.** $x = 0$ or 24

Page 93 Solving Absolute Value Equations

1. $x = 33$ or -11 **2.** ϕ **3.** $x = 11$ or -25 **4.** $x = 11$ or -29 **5.** $x = -9$ or 17 **6.** $x = 3$ or -17 **7.** $x = 19$ or -13 **8.** $x = 8$ or 2 **9.** ϕ **10.** $x = 27$ or -45 **11.** $x = 8$ or -4 **12.** $x = 38$ or -32 **13.** $x = 2$ or -8 **14.** ϕ **15.** $x = 15$ or -1 **16.** $x = 21$ or -1 **17.** $x = 12$ or -4 **18.** $x = 2$ or -18 **19.** $x = 21$ or -35 **20.** ϕ **21.** ϕ **22.** $x = -1$ or -13 **23.** $x = 7/3$ or -5 **24.** $x = 15/7$ or -3 **25.** $x = 1$ or -4 **26.** $x = 2$ or $-8/3$ **27.** ϕ **28.** $x = 2$ or $-6/5$ **29.** $x = 4$ or $-2/3$ **30.** ϕ **31.** ϕ **32.** $x = 6$ or $-11/3$

Page 94 Solving Absolute Value Equations

1. $x = 30, x = -10$ **2.** ϕ **3.** $x = -20, x = 10$ **4.** $x = -30, x = 24$ **5.** $x = -26, x = 34$ **6.** $x = -51, x = 27$ **7.** $x = -5, x = 9$ **8.** $x = -10, x = 14$ **9.** $x = -34, x = 24$ **10.** $x = -40, x = 30$ **11.** $x = -42, x = 28$ **12.** $x = -2, x = 8$ **13.** ϕ **14.** $x = -9, x = 3$ **15.** $x = -1, x = 17$ **16.** ϕ **17.** $x = 0, x = 12$ **18.** $x = -9, x = 5$ **19.** ϕ **20.** $x = -4, x = 28$ **21.** $x = -12, x = 4$ **22.** ϕ **23.** ϕ **24.** $x = 22/5, x = -12/5$ **25.** $x = -4, x = 2$ **26.** $x = -11/3, x = 1$ **27.** ϕ **28.** ϕ **29.** $x = -9/5, x = 3$ **30.** $x = -5, x = 2$ **31.** $x = -4, x = 12/5$ **32.** $x = -3, x = 7$

Page 95 Absolute Value Inequalities

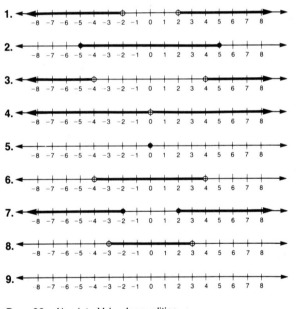

Page 96 Absolute Value Inequalities

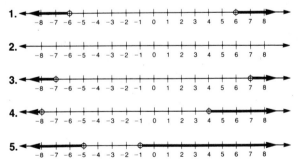

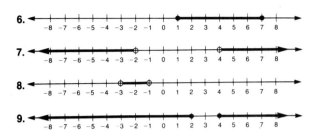

Page 97 Graphing Linear Inequalities

1. All points above the broken line going through (5, 2) and $(-2, -3)$ **2.** Solid line going through (1, 3) and $(-2, 4)$ and all points above that line **3.** All points above the broken line going through (0, 0) and (2, 2) **4.** All points to the left of the broken line going through (2, 3) and $(3, -1)$ **5.** All points to the right of the broken line going through (1, -5) and (2, 4) **6.** Solid line going through (4, -4) and $(-3, 2)$ and all points below that line

Page 98 Graphing Linear Inequalities

1. Solid line going through (1, 2) and $(-3, -3)$ and all points above that line **2.** Solid line going through (3, -5) and $(-4, 3)$ and all points above that line **3.** All points above the broken line going through (1, 2) and $(-3, 5)$ **4.** All points above the broken line going through (4, 3) and $(-5, -5)$ **5.** All points below the broken line going through (1, 3) and $(-3, 4)$ **6.** All points below the broken line going through (0, 0) and (2, -2)

Page 99 Solving Systems of Inequalities

1. 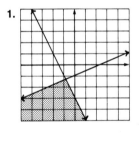 **2.**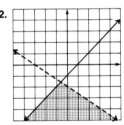

3. 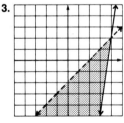 **4.**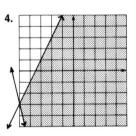

5. 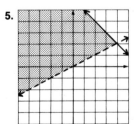 **6.**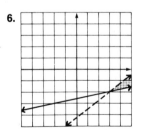

Page 100 Solving Systems of Inequalities

1.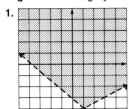

2.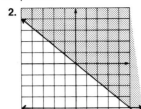

3.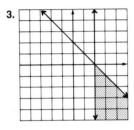

4.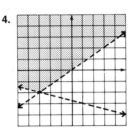

5.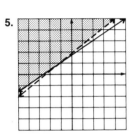

6.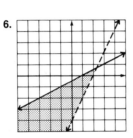

Page 101 Solving Systems of Inequalities

1.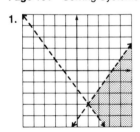

2.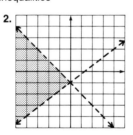

3.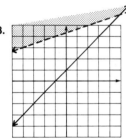

4.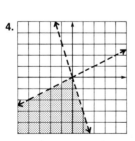

5.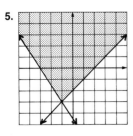

6.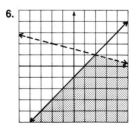

Page 102 Solving Systems of Inequalities

1.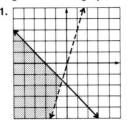

2.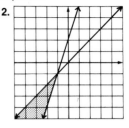

3.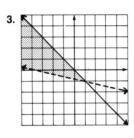

4.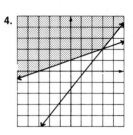

5.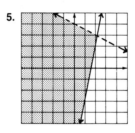

6.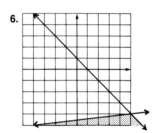

111